ART AND HISTORY IN THE OHIO JUDICIAL CENTER

ART AND HISTORY IN THE OHIO JUDICIAL CENTER

A Visual Tour

RICHARD W. BURRY

The Kent State University Press

Kent, Ohio

FOR YVONNE

ISBN 978-1-60635-465-0
Published in the United States of America

Cataloging information for this title is available at the Library of Congress.

27 26 25 24 23 5 4 3 2 1

CONTENTS

PREFACE

Some historic buildings in Ohio, like the Ohio Theatre in Columbus and the Union Terminal in Cincinnati, have a broad public reputation due to a large number of visitors. But there is one significant and remarkable building that has been largely overlooked as a landmark: the home of Ohio's highest judiciary branch. Located in downtown Columbus, sandwiched between two busy streets that parallel the Scioto River, a 15-story architectural gem hides in plain sight its treasure of abundant public art and extraordinary craftwork. This showcase of Ohio history rose from the era of the Great Depression, was completed in 1933, was fully renovated, restored, and repurposed in 2004 as the Ohio Judicial Center, and finally in 2011 was rededicated as the Thomas J. Moyer Ohio Judicial Center.

Although from a distance it's easy to overlook this apparently typical older government building, a closer look reveals numerous stone bas-reliefs on the outside and many huge murals and bronze reliefs on the inside, all depicting important persons and scenes of Ohio history. As a photographer for several Ohio preservation groups, I have photographed many hundred-year-old Ohio buildings, but the majesty and the history in this Ohio building is second only to the Ohio Statehouse.

After visiting the Ohio Judicial Center several years ago, I sought and was granted permission to come in and take photographs. Then, two years and thousands of photos later, I began looking in books and articles for information about the building's amazing art. I located a booklet, available in the Ohio Judicial Center and online, containing photographs and descriptive text. It was a disappointment to find that, otherwise, the only available information on the Thomas J. Moyer Ohio Judicial Center was one brief article in the Ohio Historical Society magazine, *Timeline*, titled "Ohio's Pride, the Art and Architecture of the Ohio State Office Building," by Barbara Powers (vol. 23, no. 1 [2006]: 2–19). A further disappointing surprise was that this building is not listed in photographic compendia of great Art Deco buildings in Ohio or America. I could not understand how a building that was so abundant in Art Deco works had remained unrecognized.

Thus began this project of creating a book to address the near void of available publications on the Thomas J. Moyer Ohio Judicial Center and its exemplary art. My photographs focus on the building's many works of art that were completed by 1933; my text supplements with anecdotes of Ohio's history and some of the backstories of the contributing artists and artisans. My hope is that this building, which exudes so much character and contains a significant collection of period art, will now claim its proper place in history for having captured Ohio's story through a snapshot of its people's lives and values in the 1930s. In preparing this book, I chose to include the history portrayed in the art and discuss how various pieces of art came to be included in the structure. Each chapter covers an individual room or part of the building and thus comprises a tour of the many and varied art styles inside and outside its walls. In discussing the Indigenous people, many terms are used: *Native Americans, Indigenous Americans,* or *American Indians.* For this book, the term *American Indian* will be used, and when possible, specific names of tribes will be included.

In the 1930s, public art was routinely included in such structures as post offices, government buildings, and schools. Some people at the time could readily identify with the depicted historical representations and relate to the progress made since Ohio was settled. Today, it is less common for public art to be included in public buildings, but we can still look at the Ohio Judicial Center's art as a lasting expression of how its artists viewed Ohio's story. We are also left with a mystery, however. We know almost nothing of how and why the planners and artists involved in building the Ohio Judicial Center chose the historic events and personages depicted. These decisions were made almost 100 years ago and were not well documented.

That leaves us with the need to review issues and politics from a century ago and even earlier. Thus, the first two chapters of this book supply the background of politics and architectural trends leading up to the Great Depression. Subsequent chapters highlight various rooms and areas within the building.

Architecture itself is a three-dimensional art form with lighting and spatial flows that change as we move within it. Let this book take you back in time to the year 1933, when the Thomas J. Moyer Ohio Judicial Center was completed. Then, find a way to come in person to visit the building and see for yourself.

Richard W. Burry, PhD
May 2023

INTRODUCTION

Architecture captures the sum of the materials, craft, art, and vision that often outlive all of the artisans who participate in a structure's creation. Completed in March 1933, the Ohio State Departments Building was designed to illustrate Ohio's history and what, a century ago, was Ohio's present.

This building has also been known variously as the Ohio State Office Building, the Departments of State Building, the Ohio Departments Building, and the State Office Building. The renovation completed in 2004 restored its original grandeur (FIG. INTRO-1) and repurposed the building's function to the home of the Ohio judiciary. Thus, the building was renamed the Ohio Judicial Center.

During the renovation, the art, walls, floors, and ceilings were brought back to their original vibrancy, with virtually nothing changed except for the addition of a half dozen judicial artworks. In 2011, after the death of Ohio Supreme Court Chief Justice Thomas J. Moyer, a strong proponent for moving the Ohio judicial function to this building, it was renamed the Thomas J. Moyer Ohio Judicial Center. However, for the rest of this book, the name Ohio Judicial Center will be used.

Today, the Ohio Judicial Center houses the Supreme Court of Ohio and its administrative offices as well as its Judicial College, Board of Professional Conduct, law library, Court of Claims, and other legal offices. The judges, attorneys, and administrators who come to the building enter through its heavy brass doors and move into the grand concourse, with its metal reliefs of past presidents. To reach other levels, they then take the elevators, whose doors are adorned with depictions of Greek history. Passing these inspiring works invokes the dignity and respect due the law and the judicial system. Such unique architectural art speaks to the enduring majesty of the building.

Fig. Intro-1. The white marble exterior of the Ohio Judicial Center from the Scioto River, looking east with downtown Columbus, Ohio, behind.

When considering why this building was erected, it is helpful to remember that by the early 1900s, Ohio's industrial expansion necessitated more government office space to keep pace with the state's expanding population. At the end of the Civil War, Ohio's population was under three million. But by 1920, the population was approximately six million, and for the first time, more people lived in cities than in rural areas. Planning for the building began in the 1920s, but construction stalled until 1930, when the construction effort became an important way to employ Ohio citizens and thus support the state's economy during the Great Depression. Construction was funded by the State of Ohio, without using either New Deal or Works Progress Administration (WPA) funds. Besides the needed office and meeting space for state agencies, the anticipated building would become home to the State Library of Ohio, which held records and proceedings from state agencies. By 1930, the building's visionaries also wanted to create a public building with distinctive architectural detailing and public art that would allow visiting citizens to share a sense of pride in their state and its history (FIG. INTRO-2).

In the 1920s when the Ohio Judicial Center was conceived, national culture and politics were complex. The Great War (World War I) ended in 1918 and signaled a victory celebration. But neither the nation nor Ohio were ready for large numbers of veterans to return into the work force. Although Ohio was growing, there were few jobs, and wages were low. This situation further fueled the existing labor union movement, resulting in numerous worker strikes at plants and at construction sites.

During the presidency of Woodrow Wilson (1913–1921), particularly following the extreme nationalism in America during World War I and the news of the Russian Bolshevik Revolution of 1917, the American mood became inward and isolationist. Many people feared Bolshevik communists and their potential infiltration into American society. During these years, known as the Red Scare, many American citizens were arrested as a result of government policies directed against protesting workers and strikers. Union workers were considered socialists, communists, or fascists, while politicians and capitalists were seen as uncaring tycoons.

Another major issue during this epoch was the influenza (the so-called Spanish flu) epidemic of 1918, which lasted three years, killing 675,000

Fig. Intro-2. Recess off the grand concourse on the east side of the first floor, an example of the outstanding design, remarkable materials, and meticulous workmanship.

Americans and causing great fear of the contagious virus. With President Wilson's nationalistic focus at the time on winning the war, and newspapers prohibited from reporting on the influenza, the resulting lack of information caused many people to panic as their neighbors died.

Another big social issue was temperance. Prohibition was enacted in 1919 as the Eighteenth Amendment to the US Constitution. It outlawed the making and selling of alcoholic beverages. Strong support came from the Women's Christian Temperance Union formed in Ohio in 1875. Resistance came from the "Wets"—breweries and people who wanted beer, wine, and liquor to remain available. Without the federal or local money needed to effectively enforce the law, many people consumed alcohol anyway. Thus arose the speakeasy culture and the motto "live for today," which characterized the roaring twenties.

Also during 1920, women voted for the first time as a result of adding the Nineteenth Amendment to the US Constitution after the emergence of the women's suffrage movement. Suffragettes wanted equal rights but had to settle for the right to vote. Much of the opposition to suffrage advocated for a return to the values of the past, since many Americans were upset by the growth of industry, the loss of agricultural jobs, and the loss of traditional lifestyles.

Warren G. Harding (1921–1923) from Marion, Ohio, followed Wilson as president. One of Harding's main campaign themes was a "return to normalcy," getting the country back to business after the extremes of the Wilson presidency. Harding was very popular and won by a landslide, with 60 percent of the popular vote. Harding relied on his cabinet for decision-making support, and one of its members, Herbert Hoover, eventually became the US president. However, another member, Harding's secretary of the interior, Albert Fall, leased the Navy oil reserve in Wyoming called Teapot Dome to a private oil company, having received a large bribe. Harding's presidency was short; he died of heart failure in his first term, and after his death, the press targeted him as responsible for the Teapot Dome scandal.

The rise and popularity of the Ku Klux Klan (KKK) brought the racial segregation issue into focus. In Ohio, with an estimated 400,000 KKK members, newspaper photographs documented Ohio parades of KKK members dressed in full regalia. The Klan members were against not only Black people but also Jews, Catholics, and anyone considered immigrants.

While the societal upheaval of the 1920s was taking place, very little happened to the plans for a new state office building. Planning finally took hold in 1929, when Ohio Governor Myers Cooper (1929–1931) authorized the Ohio State Office Building Commission to find a building site and an architect for the project. The five-person Ohio State Office Building Commission considered many building sites in Columbus, finally selecting land on the Scioto River, in part because doing so would allow the City of Columbus to remove dilapidated riverfront buildings damaged by the great flood of 1913.

These many issues set the stage for a divided country. Citizens debated and protested on all sides of them. Yet, popular culture was looking for something to believe in, something other than the problems of the day. For many, reassurance came in the form of movies and in satisfying their desire to step into the world of the rich and the famous. Seeing photos and reading about actors and notorious people's lives was one way of detaching from the troubles of the day-to-day life.

Public art provided another type of release to those who, walking into government buildings such as post offices and schools, saw the world through historical scenes and creative works. The Ohio Judicial Center's exterior and interior details depict history and the proud accomplishments of Ohio industries, transportation, and agriculture as of 1933. Imagine the impact, during the Depression, of walking into the museum-like Ohio Judicial Center and taking in all of its modern decorations and colorful art. Being in the building could give people a sense that they were part of a significant story and legacy. The art in the Ohio Judicial Center included 80 murals, 59 stone bas-reliefs, 72 metal bas-reliefs, and 15 mosaics for public viewing.

Harry Hake of Cincinnati was selected as the architect. In July of 1930, Hake presented the Commission with his final plan (FIG. INTRO-3). Educated and trained in Beaux Arts architecture at the Ohio Mechanics Institute and the Art Academy of Cincinnati, Hake had worked as a draftsman for three different architects: William Martin Aiken, Lucian F. Plympton, and George

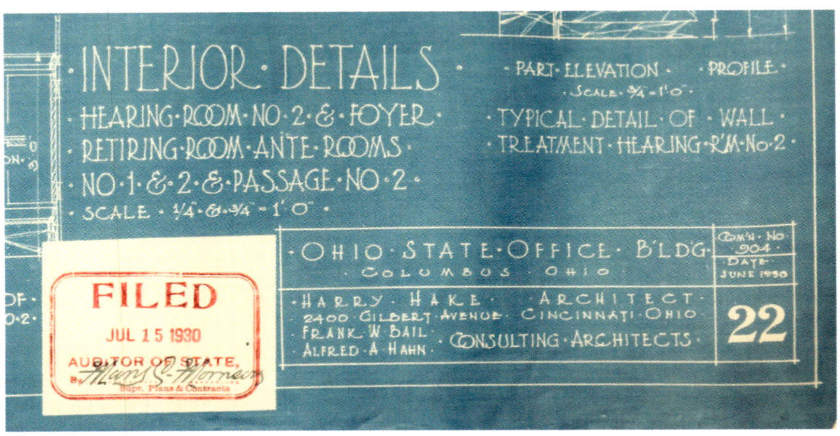

Fig. Intro-3. A lower right corner detail in the original drawings for the Ohio Judicial Center with a filing date of July 15, 1930.

W. Rapp. Hake started his own firm in 1897, and it continued through three generations of Hakes until 1971. For the Ohio Judicial Center building, Hake chose a Beaux Arts style influenced by the industrial, streamlined aesthetic of Art Deco. Hake had already designed commercial buildings, such as the Cincinnati and Suburban Telephone Company Building, using some of the same decorative design elements.

Hake's plans allocated many spaces for art such as bas-reliefs, mosaics, and murals, but he rarely added specific details. Art locations were indicated on the drawings by generic symbols, though in some cases, Hake's notes described what he envisioned as the subjects and themes for particular groups of art. Recognizing the inherent difficulty with art elements, and the obvious need for managing the artists and installation of their works, the Ohio State Office Building Commission, at its first meeting, appointed their member William F. Wiley to be a committee of one "to prepare suitable symbolisms, legends and murals and other decorations, etc. for the building, and that he selects such persons as he may require to assist him."

Thus, Wiley, with little background in public art, was put in charge of the public art and the artists who were needed to create it. Wiley was the publisher of the *Cincinnati Enquirer* and a prominent civic leader in Cincinnati. There are no records of how Wiley worked with the artists, such as how much freedom the artists had in deciding what to include or other the details of their works. We are left to look at the art and ponder what exactly the artists were told, what directions they were given, and how much personal license they had in the times and places they portrayed (FIG. INTRO-4). Further, the art gives no indication of a single, central theme or topic for the artists to portray. As a result, when walking in the building, the public art is different from room to room and area to area. It's like walking through a museum where each room or area depicts a different style or era. We are thus left with a mystery as to how the artists were inspired and directed (FIG. INTRO-5).

The Ohio Judicial Center today challenges the viewer to not only understand its art from a current perspective but also to see it through the eyes of those living almost a century ago. What did people in the 1930s think of this new futuristic building? How did the artists see their lives and the events around them? The artists' works provide us with a narrative that still speaks to us visually, with their distinctive ideas, observations, and opinions in their original places.

Above: **Fig. Intro-4.** Detail of the center of the south wall mural from hearing room 102, showing various modes of transportation and familiar Columbus buildings, including the Ohio Statehouse, LeVeque Tower, and the Ohio Judicial Center.

Left: **Fig. Intro-5.** Decoration over a drinking fountain off the grand concourse on the first floor.

ART DECO

Great buildings are more than bricks, stones, and metal. They have a story. The story can be read in how the design of the building conveys emotions and movement. The story in a building can also be read in its art and craftwork. The style of the Ohio Judicial Center is simultaneously simple and breathtaking, because it was shaped by both Beaux Arts and Art Deco.

The architect, Harry Hake, received a customary late-nineteenth-century education that emphasized the Beaux Arts style, which originated in France before becoming an important American style. Beaux Arts architecture had much ornamentation, with a classical inspiration from the Greeks and Romans. Buildings exhibited symmetry and proportion, featuring spacious common areas and lavish decoration. Floors were often terra-cotta or mosaic. Walls were covered with marble, wood panels, tapestries, or fabric. Ceilings had coffers, garlands, and frescos with gold leaf–gilded trim. Interiors sometimes included extensive decoration with flowers, Greek figures, and shields. Exteriors frequently had multiple setbacks, columns, and dramatic flattop roofs. Beaux Arts buildings were made of flat stone, often limestone, with bronze decorations and bronze doors. The style was intended to communicate the building's purposes through sculpture, symbols, sayings, and mythological figures.

Starting in the 1920s in America, the dramatic Art Deco style became popular. Art Deco flourished in America only until the mid-1930s and was

Fig. 1-1. Ceiling light in hallway off the grand concourse first floor.

Fig. 1-2. Sculpture facing Front Street on the northeast corner, with Art Deco style in smooth surfaces and sharp straight lines with strong symmetry.

seen as an expression of the technological progress of the mechanical age. Art Deco, with its simpler and abstract designs, resisted a clear-cut definition. It was a rebellion against traditional forms of architecture like Beaux Arts.

Actually, Art Deco is more of a decorative style than an architectural type, as it relies on unique designs for windows, doors, and building surfaces, rather than centering on the design of buildings. The sleek machines of the early 1920s, with their metal surfaces and minimal amount of decorative design, inspired the style (FIG. 1-1).

Art Deco style often involved shapes, textures, colors, and materials. Murals and sculptures used simple sweeping lines to show activity (FIG. 1-2). In an Art Deco building, we see Greek gods dressed in simple flowing wraps, signifying a love for the greatly revered classical past. Unadorned areas in Art Deco buildings established interest through the contrast of walls with floor or ceiling, combined with colors and textures. A strong part of any Art Deco building is the use of metal as a decorative element for doors, door frames, and lighting.

During the 1930s, most American Art Deco buildings were commercial. There were relatively few government buildings in the Art Deco style, but a great example is Nebraska's capital in Lincoln.

The 22-floor Nebraska State Capitol building in Lincoln was constructed from 1922 to 1932, with a huge metal statue of a figure sowing grain atop the building. The building, by architect Bertram Goodhue, tells the story of Nebraska's history. Its use of stone reliefs, murals, and mosaics for representing the symbolism of the building's home state was similar in style to that of the Ohio Judicial Center. But, as it is located in Nebraska, the building shows the lives of western settlers and the American Indians of the sweeping plains. A lack of funds due to the Depression meant that only external sculptures and

several inside murals were done by 1932 when the building was completed. The remaining twenty murals were completed from the 1950s to the 1990s. Thus, the building's artwork was done in different styles and shows a variety of historical viewpoints from 1932 to more recent times. The Ohio Judicial Center in Columbus is a better example of government Art Deco style, because all of its artwork was completed by 1933 and thus reflects a view from a single historical period of time.

Fig. 1–3. The east-facing front of the Union Terminal in Cincinnati, Ohio, with Art Deco–style walks and water elements. The terminal has large, smooth surfaces with sharp, distinctive lines for contrast.

There are two other great Art Deco buildings in Ohio that further demonstrate the style: Cincinnati's Union Terminal and the Carew Tower–Hilton Cincinnati Netherland Plaza Hotel. Construction of Union Terminal's quarter dome, with the contrasting flat front, began in 1929 and was completed in 1933 (FIG. 1–3).

The Union Terminal is historically important, because it united for the first time seven different railroad companies to serve one terminal, rather than each having its own. The New York architectural firm of Fellheimer

Fig. 1-4. One of the two large mosaic murals inside the half dome of the Union Terminal in Cincinnati, Ohio.

Facing page: Fig. 1-5. The Carew Tower is the taller building to the left, with the Netherland Hotel shorter and to the right in downtown Cincinnati, Ohio.

and Wagner (1928–1933) designed the Cincinnati Union Terminal as well as other railroad terminals. In addition to the curved lines of the building, the garden in front has water elements that show the smooth, curved style of Art Deco and avoidance of extensive detail (FIG. 1–3). The interior of the half dome has a simple mosaic and paint mural showing the history of transportation. The artist was German-born Winold Reiss, who was also famous for his many portraits of American Indians (FIG. 1–4).

The Carew Tower and Hilton Netherland Plaza Hotel complex in Cincinnati, Ohio, (FIG. 1–5) was built from 1929 to 1931 with funding from commercial sources. The Carew Tower has office space, with an internal mall of shops on the ground and first floor. The Netherland Hotel is a shorter building that functions as a premier hotel and has a multistar restaurant.

Inside the hotel building, the Art Deco–style decorations are based on classical Greek and Roman scenes and figures. The Palm Court is a large two-story interior space decorated in wood, stone, and murals (FIG. 1–6). Originally used as the lounge and lobby of the hotel, today it is an exquisite restaurant and elegant bar.

macy's

Fig. 1-6. The Netherland Hotel with the Orchids Restaurant at Palm Court in the foreground and the oval bar in the background, showing the use of large solid-wood panels with metal sconces and the simple lines of the ceiling, with large-framed murals at the tops of the walls.

Facing page: Fig. 1-7. Light fixture and metal artwork in the Orchids Restaurant of the Netherland Hotel.

Throughout the first three floors of the Netherland Plaza Hotel are numerous light fixtures and grills that recapture the stunning feel of the 1930s Art Deco style (FIG. 1–7). In other rooms, there are faux windows resembling ship portholes and ceiling murals of Roman gods.

SOLDIERS AND SETTLERS

Early explorers, pioneers, and settlers traveled west of the Appalachian Mountains in search of land and new home sites in what became Ohio. Hardships included primitive living, initially, like eating berries and squirrel while living in tents or log houses and traveling on muddy dirt paths. Over the years, strong men and women came to Ohio by the thousands and established towns and a new way of life. Then in the late 1800s and early 1900s, the Ohio industrial expansion began, fueled by many entrepreneurs. Working in Ohio towns, these industrial enterprises formed a dramatic contrast to the early hardships faced by settlers. The industrial revolution included machines that were able to accomplish the work of a settler in a fraction of the time. By the 1920s, Ohioans largely felt a sense of pride for the local, industrial advances.

In the early twentieth century, brave soldiers from Ohio were called to battle. They participated in large numbers and served proudly. In 1918, the "War to End All Wars" (WWI) had ended, with many Ohio soldiers dead and wounded; the loss was felt throughout the state. To show the strength of Ohio's commitment to honoring soldiers and veterans, the architect of the Ohio Judicial Center chose to designate some of the of building's exterior art to those who have served and died for America. Brave soldiers of all wars are honored for establishing and protecting the land that is now the State of Ohio.

Above: Fig. 2-1. The white marble Ohio Judicial Center looking east across the Scioto River. The exterior at the ground, first, and second floors is decorated with bas-reliefs and inspirational sayings, and behind is the 15-story building.

Right: Fig. 2-2. Plan of the first floor, showing the north pylon, middle façade, and south pylon.

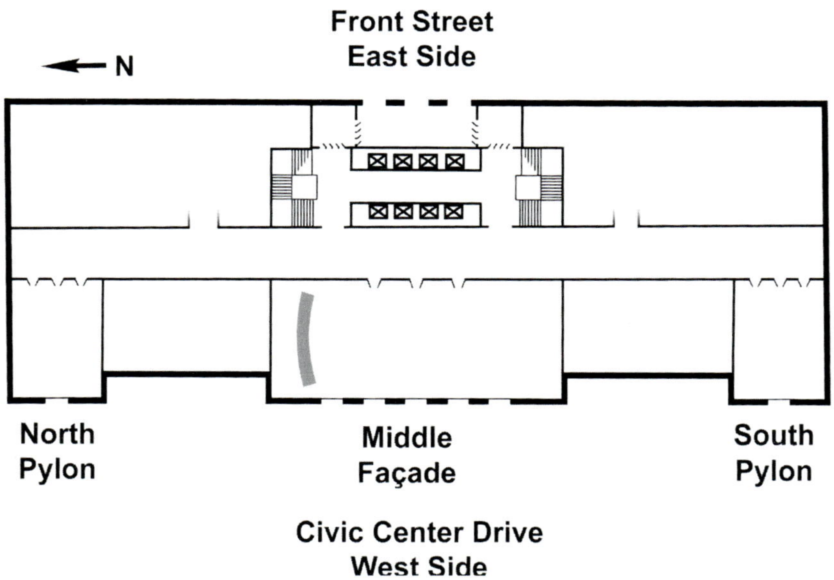

The exterior façade of the west or Civic Center Drive side of the Ohio Judicial Center is three stories tall, with the rest of the 15-story building set behind it (FIG. 2–1). This western exposure has both a north pylon and a south pylon, with a middle façade extending outward and recessed areas in between (FIG. 2–2). The three-story exterior contains bas-reliefs highlighting and honoring Ohio's early settlers and Ohio's veterans.

The stonework on the Ohio Judicial Center exterior is by sculptor Alvin Meyer. Born in Illinois in 1892 of German immigrants, he studied at the Maryland Institute for the Promotion of the Mechanic Arts in Baltimore and the Pennsylvania Academy of the Fine Arts in Philadelphia. Finishing his studies at the American Academy in Rome, Meyer went on to win the Prix de Rome in 1926. By 1929, Meyer had moved to Chicago and was

Fig. 2–3. North pylon of the building exterior on the west side facing Civic Center Drive.

director of the sculpture department at the famous Chicago architectural firm of Holabird and Root.

On the Civic Center Drive side of the building, the north pylon features pioneers of the Northwest Territory with bas-reliefs and inspirational quotations (FIG. 2–3). Over the first-floor window in the north pylon is inscribed, "Their gift to posterity a rich heritage." At the ground-floor level,

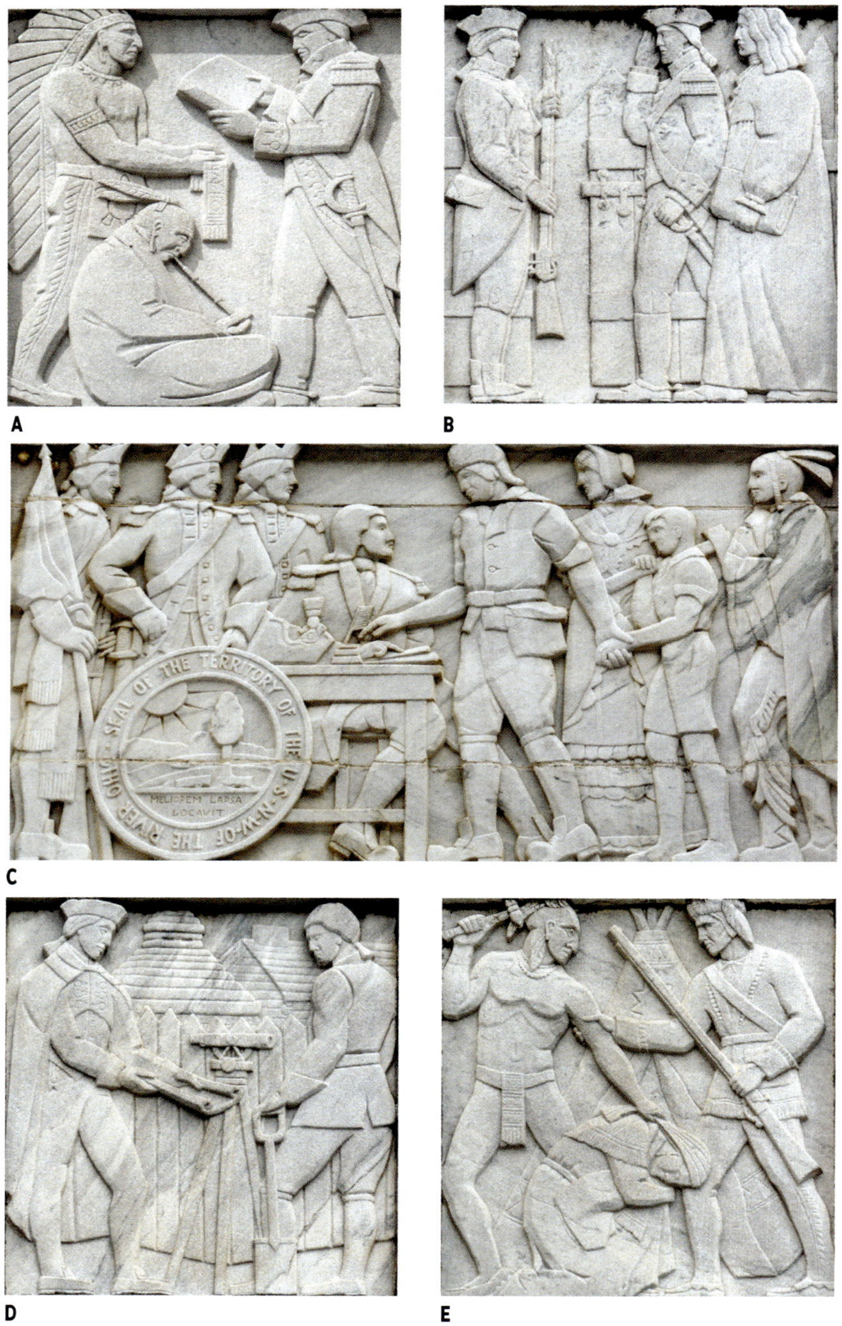

Fig. 2–4. Stone bas-reliefs on the north pylon honor the pioneers of the Northwest Territory. *A*, "Greenville Treaty"; *B*, "Campus Martius"; *C*, "Establishment of Civil Government at Marietta"; *D*, "Ft. Washington"; *E*, "Bouquet's Expedition." The titles listed are those from above the stone bas-reliefs and have not been edited.

below the windows is a long marble bench with the inscription "They raised a standard to which the wise and honest can repair" (FIG. 2–3). There is no record of who wrote the inscriptions or how they were selected.

There are five panels carved on the sides of the north pylon: one on its north side, three on its west side, and one on its south side. On the north-facing side is a single bas-relief representing the Treaty of Greenville (FIG. 2–4A), signed one year after American soldiers defeated American Indians in the Battle of Fallen Timbers in August 1794.

In 1787, the US Congress of the Confederation enacted the Northwest Ordinance for settling of land west of the Appalachian Mountains and north of the Ohio River—the Northwest Territory. The larger relief over the west-facing window shows a family of settlers and a group of soldiers standing behind a desk (FIG. 2–4C). The west-facing panels of the north pylon depict the town of Marietta, Ohio, a community established in 1788 by settlers from Boston in a part of the Northwest Territory that would become Ohio. With the threat of hostilities, a large stockade was built at the town center and called Campus Martius, "field of Mars," in typical New England style (FIG. 2–4B). In December of 1788, a group of investors

Fig. 2-5. South pylon on the west side facing Civic Center Drive.

purchased land in the Northwest Territory near the mouth of the Greater Miami River as it flows into the Ohio River. Here, at Fort Washington, they established Losantiville, as seen on the west-facing panel (FIG. 2–4D). Subsequently, the town of Losantiville was renamed Cincinnati.

The south-facing side of the north pylon depicts the end of the French and Indian War in 1763, when the American Indians resisted British oc-

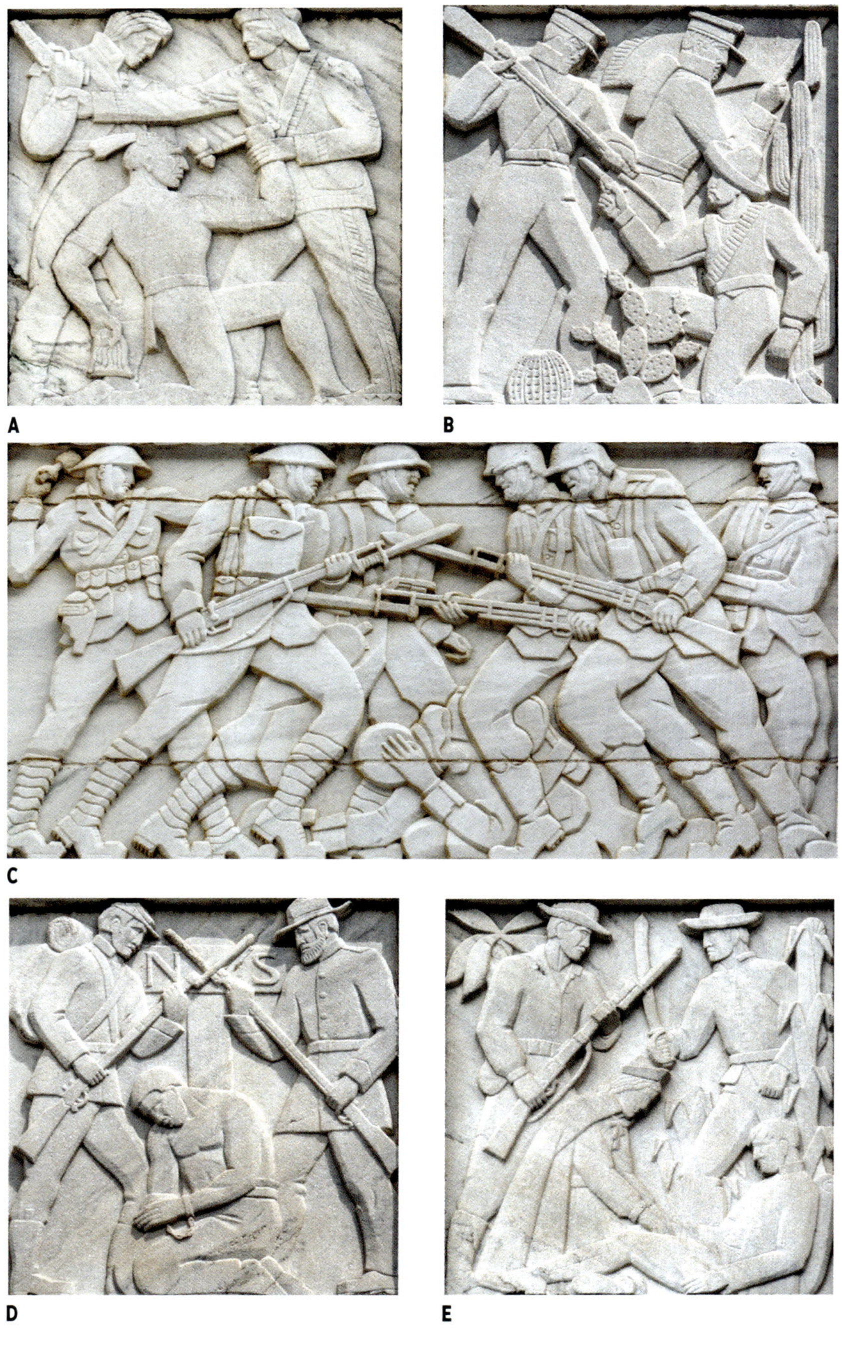

Fig. 2–6. Stone reliefs on the south pylon honoring Ohio veterans of the different wars. *A,* "England 1812"; *B,* "Mexico 1846"; *C,* "Cataclysm of Nations"; *D,* "Civil Strife 1861"; *E,* "Spanish 1898." The titles listed here are those from above the stone bas-reliefs and have not been edited.

A

B

Fig. 2–7. The first French and English adventurers, marble bas-reliefs on the north end of the building. *A,* "Céloron de Bienville"; *B,* "Pickawillany." Titles of the stone bas-reliefs listed here are from above each relief.

cupation of their land. A large confederacy of tribes, led by Chief Pontiac of the Ottawa tribe, had many skirmishes with the settlers in what has become known as Pontiac's War (FIG. 2–4E). In the end, British Colonel Henry Bouquet was successful in negotiating peace.

The south pylon has five carved panels focused on Ohio war veterans: one on its north side, three on its west side, and one on its south side (FIG. 2–5). The inscription on the west side of the south pylon above the first-floor window reads, "Their sacrifice a guarantee to posterity." On the ground level, below four windows is a bench with the inspirational saying "They set the cause above renown and met the foe with fearless eye." Early America had many reasons for instability and therefore a great need for patriotic, inspiring statements.

The north side of the south pylon depicts the War of 1812, sometimes referred to as the second American revolutionary war (FIG. 2–6A). Americans fought against the British in Ohio and on Lake Erie. The west side of the south pylon shows the Mexican-American War (FIG. 2–6B), which began in 1846 when the US annexed Texas. In the large panel just above the window, World War I, here described in the panel's label as a "Cataclysm of Nations" (FIG. 2–6C), started in Europe on July 28, 1914, with the US joining the Allies in April 1917. The Civil War, here described in the label as "Civil Strife" (FIG. 2–6D), started in 1861. The south side of the south pylon shows the Spanish-American War (FIG. 2–6E), which started on April 21, 1898, when Congress under President William McKinley declared war on Spain after the explosion and sinking of the American ship, the USS *Maine,* in a Spanish Cuban harbor.

On the north end of the building at the second-floor level are two reliefs listed as "Early Claims of French and English Adventurers." The east panel has Céleron de Bienville, a French explorer who from 1743 to 1748 led an

Fig. 2-8. South end of the building with relief panels showing previous seats of Ohio state government. *A*, "Chillicothe"; *B*, "Zanesville."

A

B

expedition to claim the Ohio River Valley for France (FIG. 2–7A). The west panel on the north side shows the village called Pickawillany (FIG. 2–7B) of the Miami tribe, who in 1747 lived on the Greater Miami River in western Ohio, near today's Piqua, Ohio. The Miami tribe traded with the French until the French attacked and captured their village.

On the south end of the building are two panels representing previous seats of state government prior to the city of Columbus. The Ross County Courthouse in Zanesville (FIG. 2–8A) was the Ohio state capital from the beginning of statehood in 1803 until 1810, and then again from 1812 to 1816. Zanesville (FIG. 2–8B) was the Ohio capital from 1810 to 1812. In 1816, Columbus became the permanent capital.

On the Civic Center Drive side of the three-story extension between the pylons and the middle façade are shields representing important attributes of good citizenship (FIG. 2–9). On the north end of the space between the north pylon and the middle façade, an emblem labeled "Loyalty" shows a figure bearing the symbol of a sword in hand, possibly referring to the virtue of defending others (FIG. 2–9A). In the shield labeled "Service," a figure's open hands symbolize the values of welcoming and supporting others (FIG. 2–9B). The shield identified as "Devotion" depicts a burning log (FIG. 2–9C), a symbol of religious belief.

To the south, in the space between the middle façade and the south pylon, an owl represents Athena in an image labeled "Wisdom" (FIG. 2–9D). The symbol inscribed as "Integrity" is an ancient plumb bob (FIG. 2–9E). The squirrel, an organizer in burying nuts in the fall for finding later, is the symbol in the emblem labeled "Vision" (FIG. 2–9F). These six qualities for citizenship were viewed as very important in 1933, but the symbols today are not easily recognizable.

Fig. 2-9. Attributes of good citizenship. *A,* "Loyalty"; *B,* "Service"; *C,* "Devotion"; *D,* "Wisdom"; *E,* "Integrity"; *F,* "Vision." In order from north to south between the north pylon and the middle façade (A to C) and between the middle façade and the south pylon (D to F).

On the middle façade, carved at the top is "1803," the year of Ohio statehood, and on the south end is "1931," the year the cornerstone of the Supreme Court Building was set (FIG. 2-10). In the center, between emblems, is an inscription: "A Commonwealth Conceived and Nurtured by Strong Men."

At the top of the middle facade, between the dates and the inscription, are four carved stone rondels representing the four characteristics of good government (FIG. 2-11). The north emblem is identified as "Justice" (FIG. 2-11A), with a traditional symbol of a balance scale. The emblem labeled "Prudence" (FIG. 2-11B) displays the symbol of a staff and a snake. In the emblem labeled "Strength" (FIG. 2-11C), the quality is expressed with an image of an axe, symbolizing the physical strength needed to fell a tree. The southernmost emblem, identified by inscription as "Clemency" (FIG. 2-11D), represents its quality by a downward-pointing sword and an olive branch. Today these qualities still make good government; however, the symbols used to depict them are not easily understood.

On the middle façade, at either end near the ground level in stone pilasters, are small stone balcony-like elements adorned with eagle symbols, each displaying an attribute of good government. The eagles face the center of

A B C D

Top: Fig. 2–10. The middle façade, showing the exterior of the ground floor and first floor. At the ground floor, the façade has three brass doors, and on the first floor, there are five windows of the Supreme Courtroom. There are rondels and aphorisms above the windows.

Above: Fig. 2–11. The marble rondels at the top of the middle façade, showing four characteristics of good government, starting at the north. *A*, "Justice"; *B*, "Prudence"; *C*, "Strength"; *D*, "Clemency."

the building, and under the north eagle is the word "Freedom" (FIG. 2–12*A*), while under the south eagle is the word "Opportunity" (FIG. 2–12*B*).

The three bronze doors on the ground floor of the Civic Center Drive were designed by Alvin Meyer (p. 11) and depict events of American and Ohio history (FIG. 2–10). Covering the time span from before the arrival of the pilgrims to the Civil War, each door has ten history panels (FIG. 2–13). The bottom two sets of panels on each door are the same, but the upper six panels depict specific and varied historical events. Individual panels each have an image surrounded by outer small symbols of pioneer life (FIG. 2–14).

The events shown in these panels start at the top left of the north door (FIG. 2–15*A*) and depicts events that are easily understood or have an obvious significance. However, the panel second from the top on the right (FIG. 2–15*A4*) is labeled "J. Smith—LaSalle—DeSoto" and shows the three explorers in dress of their countries. John Smith (1607–1615) was a British colonizer of Jamestown. René-Robert Cavelier, Sieur de La Salle,

A

B

Above: **Fig. 2-12.** At the north and south ends of the middle façade on the side of the building facing Civic Center Drive are two panels displaying attributes of good government. *A,* "Freedom"; *B,* "Opportunity."

Left: **Fig. 2-13.** The middle door on the ground floor of the west side of the building, facing Civic Center Drive, with ten metal panels.

Fig. 2–14. Individual panel, from the top right of the middle door of the ground floor, bordered by a series of symbols separated by a Greek fret design.

was a French explorer traveling from Canada to the Gulf of Mexico, and Hernando de Soto was a Spanish explorer in southeastern America and Mexico. The lower right panel of the north door (FIG. 2–15A6) shows a figure labeled "Pere Jacque Marquette," a monk holding a cross. Jacques Marquette was the French Jesuit missionary who founded Sault Ste. Marie, the first town established in Michigan.

The middle door (FIG. 2–15B) shows events related to the arrival of the *Mayflower* (1620) and the establishment of British colonies. In the second panel from the top on the left (FIG. 2–15B3) is Henry Hudson, a navigator and explorer, depicted with his ship, the *Half Moon*. On the lower right panel is a stockade fence and blockhouse likely built to protect the settlers, which may be a reference to early Marietta, Ohio (FIG. 2–15B6).

The south door (FIG. 2–15C) displays scenes from the Revolutionary War through the Civil War. The second panel from the top to the left (FIG. 2–15C3) is labeled "Geo R. Clark—D. Boone." George Rogers Clark was a

Fig. 2–15. Images of Ohio history from the three doors on the west, or Civic Center Drive, side. The letter *A* indicates images from the north door, *B* from the middle door, and *C* from the south door. Images are numbered from the top left to the bottom right.

surveyor and explorer who fought in the Revolutionary War, and Daniel Boone was a pioneer and explorer.

Opening the outer bronze doors on the ground level reveals an inner door with metalwork backed by glass (FIG. 2–16). Decorating the metal grill are emblems and pictographs representing the prehistoric American Indians of the region that became the Northwest Territory. The silhouettes are extremely stylized shapes (FIG. 2–17). While these were probably inspired by artifacts, like those from the Hopewell culture, they are in the style of Art Deco.

Symbols that represent activities of the modern state in the 1930s are shown in the grillwork of the five windows of the Supreme Courtroom (FIG. 2–18). There are ten different symbols, and they are duplicated many times on the five different windows (FIG. 2–19). There is no record of the specifications for these symbols, but they clearly have a strong Art Deco style and represent important commercial activities in the state. While this set of symbols was generated almost a hundred years ago, the list represents businesses that are still important in the early twenty-first century.

The artist, Meyer, created the stone reliefs and the brass doors seen on the west side of the building. As with other art depicting history in this building, the selection of events shown in these panels is different from the work of other artists and probably a result of the artist's own choices. There

Fig. 2-16. The inner north door of the ground floor, showing three rows of metal silhouettes.

Fig. 2-17. The silhouettes on both sides of the north inner door. Symbols labeled with numbers 1 to 3 are on the left side and with numbers 4 to 6 are on the right. The letters are in rows starting at the top of the door.

are no records of how the Commission member in charge of art selection supervised the artists. It would be interesting to know who decided on the symbols and text describing government. The selection of events and people shown on the brass doors included lesser explorers, such as Daniel Boone and George Clark, but not Ohio founders or Ohio governors, nor George Washington, who was an early surveyor of Ohio.

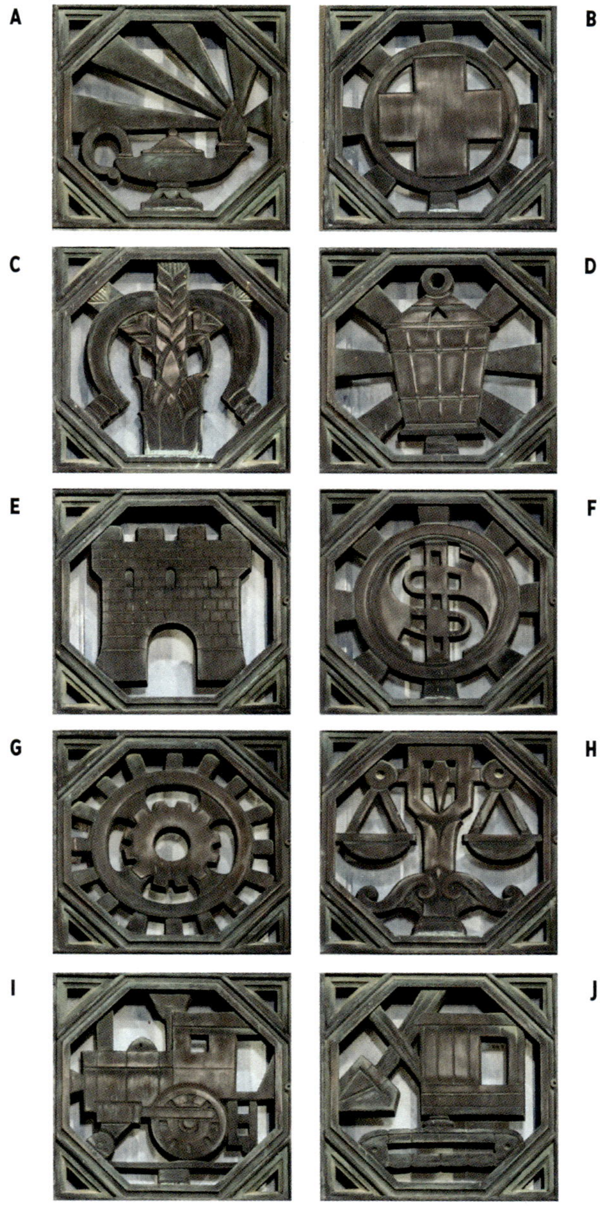

Left: Fig. 2-18. First floor middle window and surrounding grill to the Supreme Courtroom.

Above: Fig. 2-19. The Supreme Courtroom window grills showing individual symbols. *A,* "Education"; *B,* "Health"; *C,* "Agriculture"; *D,* "Religion"; *E,* "Construction"; *F,* "Banking"; *G,* "Manufacturing"; *H,* "Justice"; *I,* "Transportation"; *J,* "Construction."

3

INDUSTRY AND LABOR

In the 1920s, the Ohio economy was booming with many successful Ohio industries, which are depicted on the Front Street façade as fourteen stone bas-reliefs. Historically important industries such as transportation, agriculture, and wine-making were included, along with many new industries such as petroleum, manufacturing, and aeronautics (aviation). Jobs in these newer industries were the results of the efforts of many inventors and entrepreneurs who lived and worked in Ohio: Thomas Edison, Michael Joseph Owens, Harvey Firestone, the Wright brothers, James Murray Spangler, and Charles Kettering. Some industries such as quarrying, ceramics, mining, and founding (melting materials such as metal and pouring them into molds) are less important today, but in 1933, they were considered crucial financial activities for the state and were a source of many jobs. The bas-reliefs and sculptures on the Front Street side (FIG. 3–1) were the work of sculptor Alvin Meyer (p. 11).

Industries are named above each relief, starting at the south end of the building. The image labeled "Quarrying" (FIG. 3–2A) depicts the abundance of limestone cut from local quarries for buildings in Ohio. Shown next are "Fishing" (FIG. 3–2B) in Lake Erie and "Ceramics" (FIG. 3–2C) made with Ohio clay. "Petroleum" (FIG. 3–2D) was produced in Ohio from as early as 1860 until roughly the late 1930s.

Fig. 3-1. The east or Front Street exterior of the Ohio Judicial Center. Note the bas-reliefs above the second-floor level, and the sculptures at either end of the building.

A B C D

Fig. 3-2. The east or Front Street side with stone bas-reliefs of the industries of Ohio. *A,* "Quarrying"; *B,* "Fishing"; *C,* "Petroleum"; *D,* "Ceramics."

A B C D

A B C D

Top: Fig. 3-3. The east or Front Street side with stone bas-reliefs of industries of Ohio. *A*, "Fruit Culture"; *B*, "Aeronautics"; *C*, "Transportation"; *D*, "Manufacturing."

Above: Fig. 3-4. The east or Front Street side with stone bas-reliefs of industries of Ohio. *A*, "Construction"; *B*, "Agriculture"; *C*, "Mining"; *D*, "Live Stock."

The emblem labeled "Fruit Culture" (FIG. 3-3A) shows the work done in orchards and how it is different from agriculture or from livestock husbandry, seen in separate panels. In the panel inscribed as "Transportation" (FIG. 3-3C), the titular industry is represented by human figures moving boxes and sacks in a warehouse. "Manufacturing" (FIG. 3-3D), meaning the process of making parts individually and not on an assembly line, is also shown.

The depiction in the panel labeled "Construction" (FIG. 3-4A) includes building with stone. The illustration in the emblem inscribed as "Agriculture" (FIG. 3-4B) shows farmers broadcasting seeds and hoeing by hand. In the bas-relief labeled "Mining" (FIG. 3-4C), workers use a pickaxe and shovel coal into a cart. In the one inscribed as "Livestock" (FIG. 3-4D), workers are shown taking care of cattle and sheep.

In the bas-relief about the "Printing" industry, a foot-powered printing press is used (FIG. 3-5A). The relief labeled "Founding" (FIG. 3-5B) makes reference to Ohio coal, an important source of heat for metal castings.

The north sculpture (FIG. 3-6) highlights material and physical resources of Ohio with an American Indian holding both a gear within a gear and an ocean shell behind the head. At the base of the statue are two animals, arguably lions, panthers, or mountain lions, guarding a cornstalk. The bench below is inscribed, "The whole fabric of society rests upon labor."

Above this north statue are six figures. On the right, which is the south end, a panel with an ark and a bird represents hope (FIG. 3–7A). The middle panel features an extremely stylized flowering plant with leaves recognizable as from the buckeye, the state tree of Ohio (FIG. 3–7B). The right panel represents the theme of home by showing a fireplace (FIG. 3–7C).

A B

Fig. 3–5. The east or Front Street side with stone bas-reliefs of industries of Ohio. *A*, "Printing"; *B*, "Founding."

Fig. 3–6. Statue on the north end of the Front Street side of the building, with the cornerstone inscribed with the date "A. D. 1931" at the far right near the bottom.

A B C

D E F

A

B

Top: **Fig. 3-7.** Above the head of the north statue are panels with symbols. The southernmost symbols are *A*, "Hope," *B*, stylized Buckeye leaves, and *C*, "Home." On the north side of the statue are *D*, "Industriousness," *E*, stylized Buckeye leaves, and *F*, "Education."

Above: **Fig. 3-8.** Bas-reliefs on the south end of the north bench: *A*, "Plough and Grain"; *B*, an early "Mechanical Pump."

On the left or north side of the relief is an image of a beehive, representing industriousness (FIG. 3–7D). The middle panel shows a flower and buckeye tree leaves and is the same as the middle panel in the south set (FIG. 3–7E). In the right panel, the candle and scroll represent education (FIG. 3–7F).

At the ground level, reliefs on the ends of the bench (Fig. 3–6) show old and new ways of working: on the left, a horse-drawn plough and two bundles of harvested grain (FIG. 3–8A) and, on the right, a modern pump (FIG. 3–8B).

The south statue symbolizes the spiritual and intellectual forces in the State of Ohio (Fig. 3–9) with an American Indian woman holding a sun. The bench at the bottom of the statue contains the inscription "Education

Fig. 3-9. Statue on the south end of the Front Street side of the building.

and morality constitute the force and majesty of free government." At the statue's feet are two rams. The six symbols above the statue repeat those above the north statue, in reverse order.

The south bench is decorated with three reliefs depicting aspects of knowledge. South to north, the reliefs display representations of the arts, shown as paints and a musical instrument (FIG. 3-10A); knowledge, symbolized by books, pen, and owls (FIG. 3-10B); and the sciences, with a microscope, chemical retort flask, and chemical bottles (FIG. 3-10C).

At the Front Street entrance on the east (FIG. 3-11), the marble panels flanking the steps include the seal for the Supreme Court of the State of Ohio (FIG. 3-12). On the north side is inscribed "The Supreme Court of

A

B

C

Above: Fig. 3-10 Bas-reliefs from the south bench under the statue. *A,* "Arts"; *B,* "Education"; *C,* "Science."

Left: Fig. 3-11. Front Street entrance to the building through three portals and outer porch with doors to to the Ohio Judicial Center (not seen here) to the right and left.

Ohio," and below it, "Ohio Judicial Center." The three portals enter an outdoor porch, which is flanked by a pair of multilayered bronze lights crafted in a strongly Art Deco style.

The decorative bronze light on the south side of the portals is divided into four levels (FIG. 3-13). On the wall behind the bronze light is a metal plaque added after the building's renovation, which reads, "Erected 1931 Restored 2004." The stone relief dedication behind the light lists the people involved in construction: "Erected under authorization of the eighty eighth General Assembly of the State of Ohio. Construction began December 1930 in the administration of Governor George White. This site was chosen and this building erected by the Ohio State Office Building Commission. Carmi A. Thompson, William F. Wiley, William Green, Elmer S. Landes, Warner P. Simpson, Harry Hake Architect, Frank W. Bail—Alfred A. Hahn Consulting architects, Gilbert Bettman—Attorney General, Earl C. Shively—Assistant Attorney."

Behind the north light (FIG. 3-14) is a metal plaque and a poetic inscription: "May the lightnings of heaven which scathe and the whirlwind

Above left: Fig. 3-12. Seal of the Supreme Court of the State of Ohio on the Front Street entrance to the Ohio Judicial Center.

Above center: Fig. 3-13. Bronze decorative light to the south outside the first-floor entrance from Front Street.

Above right: Fig. 3-14. Bronze decorative light to the north outside the Front Street entrance.

Right: Fig. 3-15. Front Street south entrance door to the Ohio Judicial Center, with decorative windows at the top and four doors at the bottom.

and storm which prostrate the works of man pass by and spare this house erected by a mighty people and consecrated to social and constitutional government."

Through the portals from Front Street (FIG. 3-11) is a covered porch, and on the north and south ends are large bronze doors into the building (FIG. 3-15). Each door features vertical panels with extensive buckeye leaf patterns designed by Alvin Meyer. The buckeye tree was found widely in

Ohio and early on became a nickname for the state. The buckeye became the state tree in 1953.

The ceiling of the vestibule (FIG. 3–16) contains three American Indian–themed mosaics. Patterned with flowers, the vaulted barrel ceiling mosaics are between the marble columns. The artist who created these three mosaic panels was Rudolf Scheffler (see p. 47).

Fig. 3–16. The outdoor porch, looking directly upward to the barrel ceiling, on the Front Street side of the north entrance. The north building door is on the left, the north opening to the street is at the center top, the building wall is at the bottom, and the south building door is far to the right.

4

AMERICAN INDIAN GROUNDWORK

American Indians lived on the land that is now Ohio for thousands of years before settlers arrived. Today, we can think of this as the beginning of Ohio history. Initially, the American Indians welcomed settlers. It is poignant that the ground floor of the Ohio Judicial Center, essentially the groundwork or foundation of the building, is devoted to American Indians, who truly are the "beginning" of Ohio.

The Appalachian Mountains were a barrier for travel from the East Coast, and few settlers were able to make the journey. Early travelers in what is now Ohio were fur traders, who exchanged goods for fur pelts. Thus, explorers and traders were the primary sources of contact American Indians had with Europeans. As time passed, both the British and French thought they could colonize parts of this land, and more settlers entered, disrupting the lives of American Indians. The American Indians began resisting settlers and longing for the return of their lifeways and lands.

In the French and Indian War (1754–1763), the American Indians and the French were defeated by the British. After this loss and the inhumane treatment of the defeated Indians by the British General Amherst, King George III gave the Royal Proclamation of 1763, granting the American Indians the rights to the land west of the Appalachian Mountains, though it would be impossible to keep settlers out. Thus, American Indians saw any settler on their land as intrusion, and the settlers were often met with resistance. After the Revolutionary War, even more settlers arrived in the Ohio territory, and the American Indians did all that was possible to preserve their culture and their land. However, the settlers viewed North America as land open for the taking. The idea that settlers could freely take American Indian land was part of the settler's mindset.

As recently as the early 1900s, attitudes toward American Indians retained the belief that American expansion was justified as well as the belief that American Indians were uncivilized and unable to take care of themselves, while others considered American Indians to be "noble savages" but also fiercely warlike. The American Indians at this time were governed by the Bureau of Indian Affairs, which treated them as dependents unable to conform to American society. In some cases, their financial activities were run by appointed settler guardians, who took a large fee for spending their money.

In the Ohio Judicial Center, the amount of space on the ground floor devoted to American Indian motifs was unique for its time. Given the changing and diverse attitudes in 1933, it would be interesting to under-

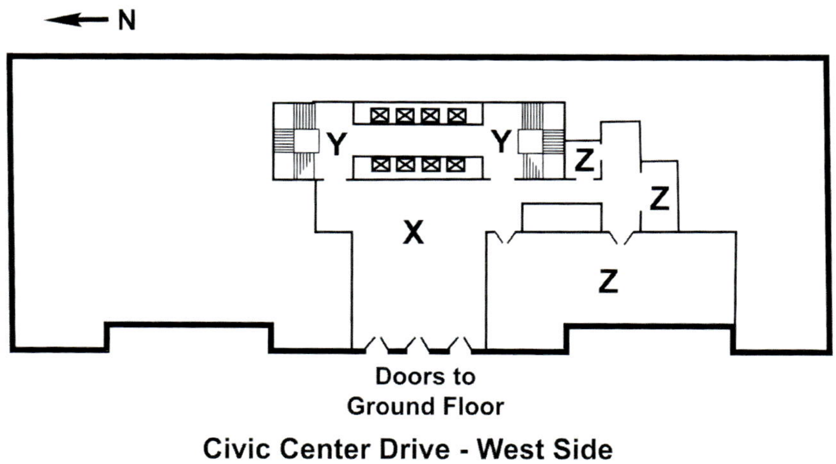

Right: **Fig. 4-1.** The ground floor of the Ohio Judicial Center. *X*, the lobby from the west entrance, *Y*, the lobby area with the grand stairs and the lobby for the eight elevators; *Z*, visitor education center areas.

Below: **Fig. 4-2.** Ground floor lobby, from the west entrance, showing concave mosaic ceiling and bas-reliefs of American Indians leaders.

Fig. 4-3. The mosaic ceiling between the arches, looking up from the floor. The white circle with the dot in the center is a light fixture.

stand the architect's decision to devote this much space to native cultures. Four tribal leaders were selected for the honor of recognition with bronze plaques on this floor, even if they had actively resisted the expansion of American settlers into Ohio.

The ground floor lobby, and its entrance off of Civic Center Drive, was the original entrance to the building (FIG. 4-1X), but today the main entrance is on the Front Street side. During changes to the Ohio Judicial Center in 2004, a Visitor Education Center (FIG. 4-1Z) was added to help visitors understand and experience the different functions of the Ohio judicial system (see chapter 10, p. 106).

The interior of the ground floor (FIG. 4-2) is decorated with arching ceilings, each having mosaics with traditional patterns (Fig. 4-3). The mosaics are composed of easily identifiable patterns of zigzag lines, diamonds, and other geometric shapes used by Art Deco artists as representative of American Indian designs.

Also in the interior on the ground floor are four bronze plaques of celebrated American Indian chiefs by sculptor Paul Fjelde (FIG. 4-4). Born in Minneapolis, the son of a Norwegian sculptor, Fjelde entered the Minneapolis Society of Fine Arts at fourteen. He studied at the Art Institute of Chicago, in New York, in Copenhagen, and in Paris. Fjelde held teaching positions at Carnegie Institute of Technology Pittsburgh and the National Academy of Design in New York City. He had a prolific career in metal sculpture, and his works can be found in museums and collections throughout America.

Fig. 4–4. Four bas-relief brass plaques honoring tribal chiefs. *A,* "Pontiac"; *B,* "Logan"; *C,* "Tecumseh"; *D,* "Little Turtle."

An Ottawa Chief, Pontiac (1720–1769) (FIG. 4–4A), feared that the British, having won the French and Indian War, would take land west of the Appalachian Mountains they had previously promised to the American Indians in the Treaty of Easton of 1758. Pontiac's fears became reality when the Treaty of Paris of 1763 gave this land to the victorious British. Chief Pontiac was the leading voice in the resulting rebellion of 1764, called Pontiac's War, where American Indians initially captured Fort Detroit and Fort Sandusky. The British Colonel Henry Bouquet was appointed to end the hostilities. In 1764, the fighters allied with Chief Pontiac returned to their tribes, and Pontiac negotiated an end to the conflict, but not to the American Indian resentment of intrusion by settlers.

Chief Logan (1723–1780) (FIG. 4–4B) was known as a convincing speaker and strong leader of the Seneca-Cayuga Nation. In 1774, he lived north of the Ohio River near present-day Steubenville, Ohio. Two Virginia settlers crossed the Ohio River and killed a dozen American Indians in what is known as the Yellow Creek Massacre (1774). Several of those killed were relatives of

Chief Logan. As a result, Chief Logan committed himself to revenge on all settlers and convinced many among his people to join him. The raids into Virginia caused panic among the settlers. The British governor of Virginia, John Murray, Lord Dunmore (Earl of Dunmore), brought militia troops into Ohio to stop the raids. Logan refused to participate in negotiations to end the conflict but was satisfied that he had achieved his revenge, and the raids stopped. In 1774 Chief Logan delivered a speech under a large elm tree near Circleville, Ohio, that has come to be called Logan's Elm Speech. In one part of the speech, Logan discusses relations with the Europeans: "I appeal to any white man to say that he ever entered Logan's cabin, but I gave him meat; that he ever came naked, but I clothed him. He will not turn his heel to save his life. Who is there to mourn for Logan? No one."

The Shawnee Chief Tecumseh's (1768–1813) (FIG. 4–4C) legacy is the protection of American Indian homelands and the freedom of his people. In the War of 1812, when British soldiers fought against America soldiers, Chief Tecumseh allied with the British. He led a large confederacy with the purpose of uniting tribes from the Great Lakes region and regaining their lands west of the Appalachian Mountains. Tecumseh helped the British General Isaac Brock take Fort Detroit from the Americans. But following the British defeat at the naval Battle of Lake Erie in 1813, General Brock's troops engaged the British and Indian confederacy in the Battle of the Thames. The British, with the confederation of tribes, lost the battle and retreated into southern Canada, where Tecumseh was killed in 1813 by American soldiers.

The Miami Chief Little Turtle (Mishikinakwa) (1752–1812) (FIG. 4–4D), was a strong leader and a talented military tactician. After the Revolutionary War, many settlers started moving west into the Ohio Territory, despite the British treaty giving the American Indians the land west of the Appalachian Mountains. Violence broke out in the disputed territory, and President Washington decided to send an American force to protect the settlers. In separate battles, Little Turtle defeated two American generals, Joseph Harmar in 1790 and Arthur St. Clair in 1791. Eventually, General Anthony Wayne fought and defeated the confederation of American Indian tribes at the Battle of Fallen Timbers in 1794. In the resulting Treaty of Greenville in 1795, the American Indians kept the northern third of what is now Ohio.

The American Indian leaders shown in the bas-reliefs are from the eastern forest tribes of the Northwest Territory, not from the prairie, though they are depicted here in stylized dress typical of American Indians from the plains. They were shown as similar, with strong, muscular bodies and erect posture. Such representations must be viewed as the subjective

Fig. 4-5. On the ground floor, American Indian children. The bronze relief is cut away to show the marble wall behind.

Fig. 4-6. Ground floor elevator lobby, showing the vaulted mosaic ceiling, the terrazzo floors, and the bronze and nickel elevator doors. Looking north, the stairway to the grand staircase to the first floor is visible at the end of the lobby.

creations of the artists, as other depictions of American Indians made by painters and photographers such as George Catlin, Elbridge Ayer Burbank, Gilbert Charles Stuart, and Edward Curtis show unique faces and stature. Finally, it is not known how these four leaders were selected in 1933 from all those in the Northwest Territory and the State of Ohio. In addition to the four chiefs, Fjelde also completed a cutout bronze panel illustrating American Indian children engaged in traditional crafts (FIG. 4–5).

The elevator lobby on the ground floor has eight elevator doors by Fjelde, all with the same Art Deco designs (FIG. 4–6). These elevator doors all feature an intricate American Indian–inspired pattern in the Art Deco design style, with a line in the center of the door where the doors close (FIG. 4–7).

The design on these panels uses a wide range of Art Deco interpretations of American Indian patterns (FIG. 4–8). The beauty of this design lies in how its complex pattern appears simultaneously simple. In the center, the sun, made of nickel, provides vivid contrast. Light radiates from the sun, with stylized clouds between the rays. Further out, zigzags radiate to the edge of the pattern, interspersed with shapes and textures. Although this is a circular repeated design, the pattern from the top to the bottom of the design appears different because of the angles of the light and the shadows it forms. The contrast between the lighter color of bronze and the color of the nickel sun makes the relief stand out strongly.

The ventilation grill on the ground floor is a stylized depiction of plants that were part of American Indian cultures (FIG. 4–9). The plants are tall,

Fig. 4–7. Example of a ground floor elevator door, all of which have the same appearance.

Fig. 4-8. Close view of the elevator door, showing the detailed Art Deco design with many repeated motifs around the center. The black line in the center is where the two doors meet.

with leaves growing from their stems and with the veins of the leaves parallel to their edges. Such corn and grains, related to grasses, served as a major source of food for American Indians. The plants shown on this grill also have a flower at the top that could be from a flowering plant other than a type of grass or corn. The three plants are cast in bronze, and the casts are held by straight frames made from contrasting cut metal stock. Regardless of the identification, the plants in the unusual, stylized metal work are a great example of how the Art Deco artists used American Indian art as an inspiration for their work.

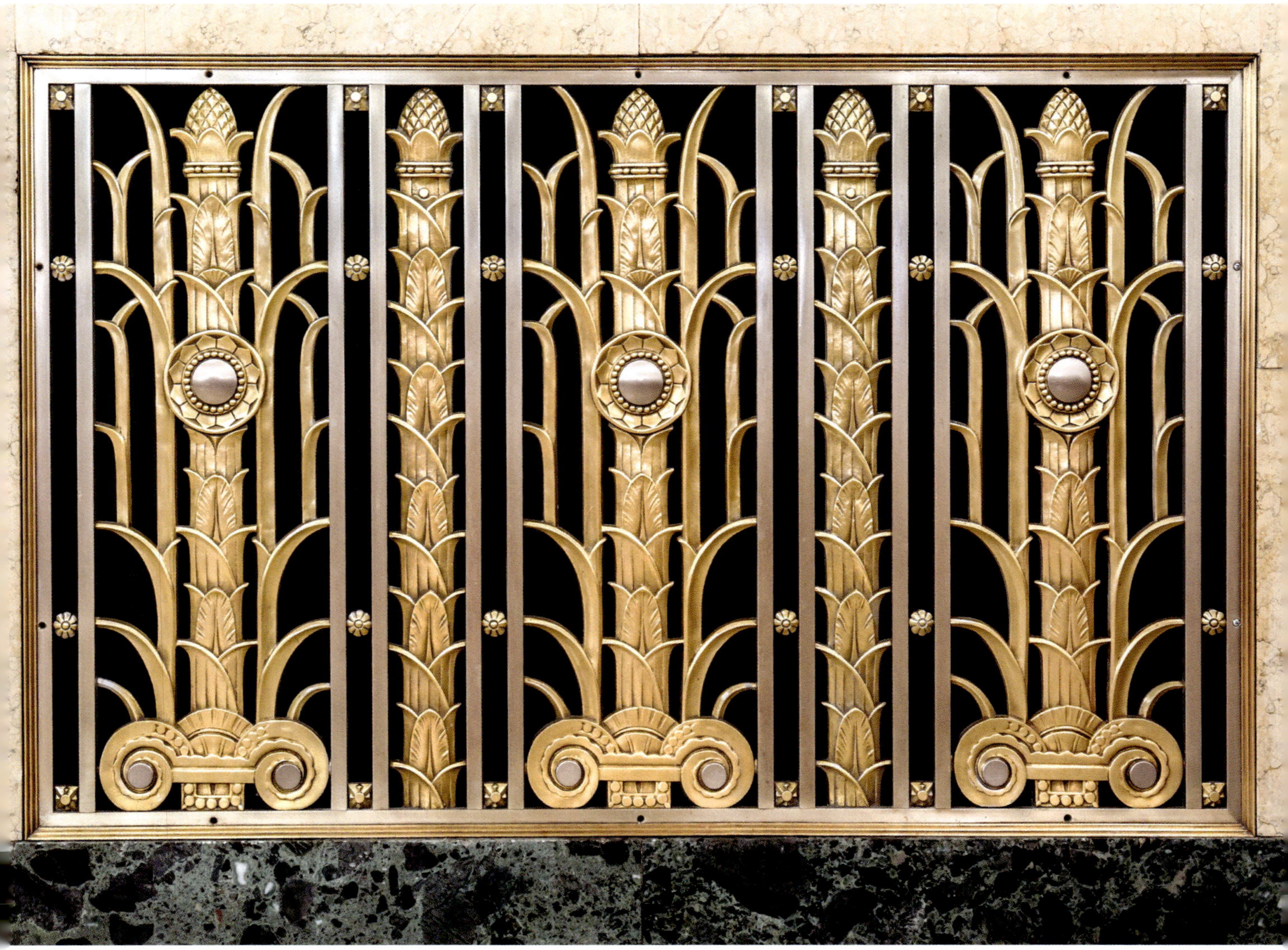

Fig. 4-9. A bronze air ventilation grill on the ground floor, with stylized American Indian symbols for corn and other plants.

HONORING THE PAST

The first-floor artwork of the Ohio Judicial Center ranges from retelling Ohio history to celebrating the tradition of the Greek and Roman ages. The entrance from Front Street through the three portals (see FIG. 3–11, p. 31) into the porch (FIG. 5–1A) opens onto the gorgeous north and south bronze doors (see FIG. 3–15, p. 32), which give access to the first-floor lobby (FIG. 5–1B), the grand stairs, the elevators, and the grand concourse (FIG. 5–1C).

At both ends of the first-floor lobby are stunning flights of marble grand stairs leading to the ground floor (FIG. 5–2, 5–3). Each stairway has a large

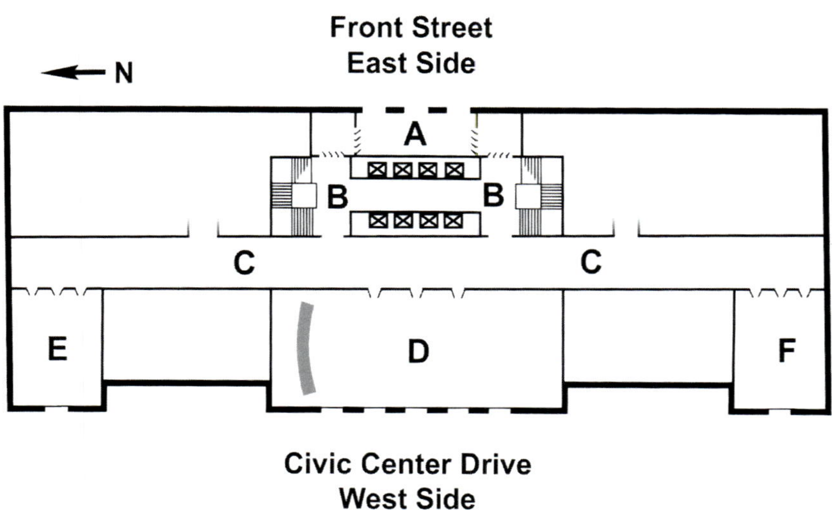

Fig. 5–1. The first-floor plan of the Ohio Judicial Center. *A*, the outdoor porch to the entrance on either side; *B*, the first-floor lobby, with the grand stairs to the ground floor and the eight elevators in the center; *C*, the grand concourse; *D*, the Supreme Courtroom, showing three doors to the grand concourse, five windows to the west exterior, and the curved justices' bench in gray to the north end; *E*, hearing room 106, the north hearing room; *F*, hearing room 102, the south hearing room.

VULCAN
HARNESSING THE ELEMENTS

CERES
FRUITS OF THE SOIL

Facing page, top left: Fig. 5-2. The north grand stairs from the first floor to the ground floor, looking to the northeast.

Facing page, top right: Fig. 5-3. The south grand stairs from the first floor to the ground floor looking to the southeast.

Facing page, left: Fig. 5-4. Mosaic of Vulcan in the north grand stairs.

Facing page, right: Fig. 5-5. Mosaic of Ceres in the south grand stairs.

This page: Fig. 5-6. Ceiling of the north lobby, with decorative painting of the directions of the compass.

mosaic by Rudolf Scheffler (1884–1973) that conveys the importance of agriculture and industry in Ohio. Scheffler was born in 1884 in Germany, educated in Dresden, Rome, and Paris, and moved to the US in 1924 at the age of 40. Scheffler is known for murals, mosaics, and stained glass in churches and public buildings throughout Europe and America. In America, he spent summers pursuing easel painting and was a member of the Old Lyme colony of artists in Connecticut. How he was selected is not known, but his established reputation was a likely factor.

The mosaic along the north grand stairs represents the strength of Ohio industry. The Roman god of fire, Vulcan, is depicted with the inscription "Harnessing the Elements" (FIG. 5–4). In the south stairway, Ceres, the Roman goddess of agriculture, is depicted with the inscription "Fruits of the Soil" (FIG. 5–5).

The ceilings of the lobbies are adorned with decorative paintings showing early systems of navigation. In the north lobby the painting shows a compass (FIG. 5–6) with winged angels blowing ram's horns to indicate directions. The style of these classical paintings is Art Deco, with simple, oval lines and mythological characters.

The south lobby ceiling features constellations used for navigation, along with symbolic representations of Greek deities and animals (FIG. 5–7). How these designs were selected is not known, but their rendering in Art Deco style seems to add height to this space with radiating lines from the center. Ceilings in both lobbies are unique to the building, because they were not murals but made with stencils used to create the differently colored shapes (FIG. 8–8). Murals in the rest of the building were done with freehand painting. Some of the design elements in the ceiling also utilize gold and silver leaf within stencils. The construction record indicates that these ceilings were contracted to the Rambusch Decorating Company of New York City.

Fig. 5-7. Ceiling of the south lobby, with decorative paintings of star constellations used for navigation.

Fig. 5-8. Mural in the ceiling of the north lobby, with a detailed view of winged angel, showing the use of stencil.

The decorative painting is different from other forms of art in the building, as the decorative paintings were not individually commissioned but painted by various artists at the direction of the decorative painting designer. Decorative painters applied designs, created faux surfaces, gilded with gold or silver, used stencils, and painted on canvas, but they were not painters of walls or ceilings. The profession of decorative painting flourished from the early 1800s until the 1930s, and today only a few companies are qualified to repair damage to these pieces. Leif Neandross of Rambusch Decorative Paint Company did the original decorative painting design from the architectural drawings. The site manager was a relative, Knud Neandross, who managed the site decorative painters. The Rambusch Decorating Company also worked on the Roxy Theatre and the Waldorf

Astoria Hotel, both in New York City, and the Ohio Theatre in Columbus, among many other buildings. When the work on the Ohio Judicial Center was stopped after an explosion that destroyed part of the ground and first floor, Rambusch had to redo the decorative paintings, but fortunately, they had not yet installed the murals at the time of the explosion. Thus, Rambusch got paid twice for a single job!

The first-floor elevator lobby walls are covered with the same marble used in the grand stairs (FIG. 5–9). Each of the eight elevator doors on the first floor has a different Art Deco classical scene in the center (FIG. 5–10). These nickel bas-relief panels represent, on the east side, the ancient theme of the four seasons and, on the west side, the four classical elements. Each individual door (FIG. 5–11) displays a different scene showing a man and a woman depicting the seasons or elements. These bas-reliefs were created by Paul Fjelde (see p. 37).

The four classical elements, north to south on the east side, include earth (FIG. 5–11A), wind (FIG. 5–11B), water (FIG. 5–11C), and fire (FIG. 5–11D). The image of water could have been intended as Lake Erie, except for the starfish in the sand above the man's right foot. The panel showing fire is

Fig. 5–9. First-floor lobby, with eight elevator doors looking to the grand staircase at the south end.

unique, as it is the only of these panels including an item from modern times: a hose and tank.

The west side's seasons are spring (FIG. 5–11E), summer (FIG. 5–11F), fall (FIG. 5–11G), and winter (FIG. 5–11H). The panel showing winter is the only one to show both figures fully clothed. In all panels, along the sides is an Art Deco border containing a relief with the same pattern of angles, arcs, and sun rays found elsewhere in the building.

The United States Post Office mailbox for the building is on the first floor between the west elevators (FIG. 5–12), with a chute connection from

Fig. 5–10. The southeast elevator door, showing a metal relief symbolizing the element of "Fire."

A

B

C

D

E

F

G

H

Fig. 5–11. First-floor elevator door reliefs. Starting at the building's north end, panels *A* through *D* are on the east side and show the four classical elements. *A*, "Earth"; *B*, "Wind"; *C*, "Water"; *D*, "Fire." Panels *E* through *H* are on the west side and show the four seasons. *E*, "Spring"; *F*, "Summer"; *G*, "Fall"; *H*, "Winter."

floors above. Although the receiving box was specified by the US Postal Service, it was customized by Fjelde to complement the building style with a highly stylized bald eagle symbolizing the US Postal Service.

The grand concourse (FIG. 5–1C) truly lives up to its name (FIG. 5–13). Two stories high, this hall runs from south to north, and its majestic space contains terrazzo floors inlayed with geometric metal patterns and colors that match the unusual blue marble of the walls. The metal bas-reliefs of prominent Ohio government officials are located high on the marble walls (FIG. 5–14). The architect, Harry Hake, made the grand concourse in the style of Beaux Arts rather than Art Deco, with a two-story-high ceiling, pilasters, and beam-like ceiling coffers.

Fig. 5–12. First-floor lobby with US Postal Service mail-receiving box on the west between the elevators. The front panel includes an Art Deco eagle.

Fig. 5-13. Grand concourse, looking north, with the portrait of Chief Justice Thomas J. Moyer on the west wall between the US and Ohio flags.

The bronze bas-reliefs in the grand concourse (FIG. 5-13, 5-14) feature prominent national officials from Ohio as of the time when the building was constructed: eight US presidents (FIG. 5-15), nine US Supreme Court justices, and two speakers of the US House of Representatives. A brief history is presented for each of the eight US presidents with roots in Ohio up to that time, from the ninth president in 1891 to the twenty-ninth president in 1921.

William Henry Harrison, the ninth president, born a British citizen in 1773 in Virginia, served in 1841 (FIG. 5-15A). He lived most of his life in Ohio. Known for his successful military battles against a confederation of American Indian tribes, he served in the US House of Representatives and the US Senate before running for president with the vice presidential candidate John Tyler. On April 4, 1841, a month after his inauguration, he died of pneumonia, and Vice President John Tyler became President. The bronze bas-relief was created by Erwin Frey.

Ulysses S. Grant was born in Point Pleasant, Ohio, in 1822 and graduated from West Point. He was the eighteenth president and served from

Fig. 5-14. View of the first-floor lobby through the entrance to the north end of the grand concourse looking east. The bronze doors in the center background are the entrance doors into the lobby. The grand staircase is to the left, and the elevators are to the right. On the ceiling is the mural of the directions of the compass. On the upper walls of the grand concourse are bronze bas-reliefs of Ohioans who served as US presidents, US Supreme Court justices and speakers of the US House of Representatives.

Facing page: Fig. 5-15. Bronze bas-reliefs of eight Ohio-based United States presidents in the grand concourse, shown in chronological order of holding office. *A,* "William Henry Harrison"; *B,* "Ulysses S. Grant"; *C,* "Rutherford B. Hayes"; *D,* "James A. Garfield"; *E,* "Benjamin Harrison"; *F,* "William McKinley"; *G,* "William Howard Taft"; *H,* "Warren G. Harding."

1869 until 1877 (FIG. 5-15*B*). A military hero in the Civil War, he served as general of the army under President Andrew Johnson after Lincoln's assassination. Grant's presidency faced strong opposition from the South and suffered several scandals during his administration. Erwin Frey prepared the bronze bas-relief.

Rutherford B. Hayes became the nineteenth president, serving from 1877 to 1881 (FIG. 5-15*C*). He was born in Delaware, Ohio, in 1822 and attended Kenyon College and Harvard Law School. As a lawyer in Cincinnati, he practiced commercial law and defended enslaved people. Hayes served in the Civil War, was elected to the US House of Representatives, and was a three-term governor of Ohio. Hayes was selected as a Republican to run for president based on his ability to unite a divided party. As he promised he would, he served one term and did not seek a second term. Mary (May) Elizabeth Cook created this bas-relief.

James A. Garfield followed Hayes as the twentieth president in 1881 (FIG. 5-15*D*). Garfield was born in 1831 in what is now Moreland Hills, Ohio. He attended Hiram College in Hiram, Ohio, and graduated from Williams College in Williamstown, Massachusetts. Then he returned to Hiram

College to teach. Garfield served in the Civil War and was elected a US representative and to the US Senate. As an abolitionist, many of Garfield's views were similar to those of Hayes. Garfield's presidency got off to a good start, but on July 2, 1881, he was shot by a disgruntled man who did not get a job in his administration. Garfield died in office, 79 days later on September 14, 1881. This bronze bas-relief was made by Mary (May) Elizabeth Cook.

Benjamin Harrison was the twenty-third president, from 1889 to 1893, and was born in North Bend, Ohio (FIG. 5–15E). He attended Miami University in Oxford, Ohio, and after graduation moved to Indianapolis, Indiana, to set up his law practice. Harrison served in the Civil War with distinction, and at the end of the war he returned to Indiana politics. After serving as a US senator, Harrison was nominated for president from a diverse field of Republicans and barely won the election against the incumbent Democratic President Grover Cleveland. Harrison ran for reelection, but he lost to the man he had defeated, Grover Cleveland. Ernest Bruce Haswell created this bronze bas-relief.

William McKinley was the twenty-fifth president, from 1897 to 1901, and was born in Niles, Ohio, in 1843 (FIG. 5–15F). McKinley attended college but dropped out to enlist in the Union Army. He was involved in several battles at the end of the Civil War. McKinley developed great political skill as a Republican US representative and as Governor of Ohio before running for president. With his outgoing personality, political acumen, and influence, he proved successful in beating the populist William Jennings Bryan. An anarchist, Leon Czolgosz, shot McKinley as he was greeting well-wishers at an exhibition. McKinley passed away on September 14, 1901, and his vice president, Theodore Roosevelt, became president. The bronze bas-relief was made by Ernest Bruce Haswell.

William Howard Taft was the twenty-seventh president, from 1909 to 1913, and subsequently a US

Supreme Court chief justice from 1921 to 1930 (FIG. 5–15G). Born in Cincinnati, Ohio, in 1857, Taft's father was in the cabinet of President Grant. Taft attended Yale and studied law at the University of Cincinnati. After serving in various positions under several presidents, Taft was selected by Theodore Roosevelt as the presidential successor, and Taft won against William Jennings Bryan in Bryan's last campaign for president. Years later, President Harding appointed Taft as a chief justice of the US Supreme Court. Erwin Frey created the bronze bas-relief.

Warren G. Harding, the twenty-ninth president, serving from 1921 to 1923, was born in 1865 in Blooming Grove, Ohio (FIG. 5–15H). Harding attended a small college in Iberia, Ohio, where he and a friend started a small weekly newspaper, the Iberia *Spectator*. After graduation, Harding moved to Marion, Ohio, and became editor of the *Marion Star*. In 1884, attending the Republican Convention as a reporter fueled his interest in politics. Harding was subsequently elected to the Ohio Senate and also served as Ohio Lieutenant Governor. In his run for president, his themes were "America First" and "a return to normalcy" after the first World War. Harding's administration made great strides in government finance and worker's rights and established the Veterans Administration, but unfortunately he is mainly remembered for the scandals in which his cabinet members were involved. On August 2, 1923, Harding died of a heart attack while on a trip to the western United States, and his vice president, Calvin Coolidge, succeeded him. This bronze bas-relief was done by Mary (May) Elizabeth Cook.

During the period of the Ohio Presidents, from the late 1800s to the early 1900s, Ohio was a major leader in industry and transportation. Many inventions and innovations of the industrial era were made or developed in Ohio. In the industrial revolution, Ohio also played a major role because of its transportation systems of roads, canals, and trains combined with its resources of energy and materials. Thus, the era of the Ohio presidents represents the state's great influence on the growth and development of America.

The artists who created the metal bas-reliefs were from or had connections with Ohio. They likely were selected by William Wiley and Harry Hake, who both had strong connections to the arts community in Cincinnati.

Mary (May) Elizabeth Cook was born in Chillicothe, Ohio. Her knowledge of human anatomy as a trained artist was put to further use in sculpting for reconstructive facial surgeries in Baltimore and Columbus hospitals following World War I. In Columbus, Cook is known for the sculpture of Peter Pan at the Metropolitan Library. For the Judicial Center, she made the bas-reliefs of Presidents Rutherford B. Hayes, James A. Garfield, and Warren G. Harding.

Erwin Frey was a native of Lima, Ohio, and born of German parents. Frey studied in New York and Paris, won several awards, and returned to head the sculpture department at the Ohio State University. His most important sculpture was the large bronze statue of William Oxley Thompson installed in front of Thompson Library on the Ohio State University's campus. He completed the bas-reliefs of Presidents William Henry Harrison, Ulysses S. Grant, and William Howard Taft.

Ernest Bruce Haswell was born in Kentucky and studied in the Art Academy of Cincinnati and at the Académie Royale des Beaux Arts, Brussels, Belgium. In the US, he was renowned for his work at the Rockwood Pottery Company in Cincinnati, Ohio. In 1932, Haswell designed the Procter & Gamble (P&G) logo, with its well-known moon and star. He made the bas-reliefs of Presidents Benjamin Harrison and William McKinley.

In the grand concourse, above each of the four east entrances, there are bronze panels with areas cut away so the marble behind is visible as the background (FIG. 5–14). The titles, in no specific order, are given in the architectural documents as *Literature, Art, Law,* and *Science* (FIG. 5–16). In these panels, people are shown in flowing gowns of classical Beaux Arts style, with Greek and Roman figures and symbols, in panels created by Ernest Haswell.

Fig. 5–16. In the grand concourse, over each of the four entrances from the east is a single bronze bas-relief with blue marble showing through. From the south to the north entrances. *A,* "Art"; *B,* "Literature"; *C,* "Law"; *D,* "Science."

A

B

C

D

Fig. 5-17. Grand concourse ceiling and upper wall, showing the Greek fret and bronze shields.

Fig. 5-18. Air ventilation grill in the grand concourse.

The southernmost panel, over the entrance to the grand concourse is, arguably, *Art* (FIG. 5–16A), and the relief that is likely titled *Literature* is above the south opening to the elevator lobby (FIG. 5–15B). A case could be made for reversing the labels of these two reliefs, because of the overlap between the symbols they contain. *Law* is the relief above the north opening into the lobby, with representations of Roman, Christian, and Jewish law (FIG. 5–15C). Science is represented by the relief above the north passage to the current Ohio Supreme Court Civic Education Office (FIG. 5–15D).

The ceiling of the grand concourse has extensive decorative painting, which includes generous amounts of gold leaf (FIG. 5–17). The ceiling beams are done in plaster and painted in shades of pink that coordinate with the pink marble on the walls. The ceiling beams contain a popular Art Deco feature, the pattern of the Greek fret, also known as the Greek key or the Greek meander. This design was found in early Greek buildings, and a meaning of unity or infinity is attributed to it.

Large grills for air ventilation in the grand concourse are covered by ornate metal work (FIG. 5–14, 5–18). The original building construction had no air conditioning, so cooling was accomplished by moving air through a network of large ventilation shafts covered with highly stylized Art Deco grills. The grills in the grand concourse are handmade from castings of plants and leaves, with metal stock for the frame elements attached between. For all of the grills in the building, we have no record of who designed or crafted them, however they would fit the abilities of Rambusch, the decorative painter.

SUPREME COURTROOM: OHIO HISTORY

The Supreme Courtroom (FIG. 6–1D) is the most ornate room in the building. Walnut paneling and red Numidian marble with dark Bois Jourdan marble give the impression of a noble space. Draperies, fabric-covered wall panels, and elements of the decor are all in reds and browns (FIG. 6–2). At the north end, behind the justices' bench, a large red curtain covers an area where, previously, officials sat at a bench, and sometimes the space was used as a film projection screen. The mural-rich ceiling with its deep coffers adds to the feeling of nobility.

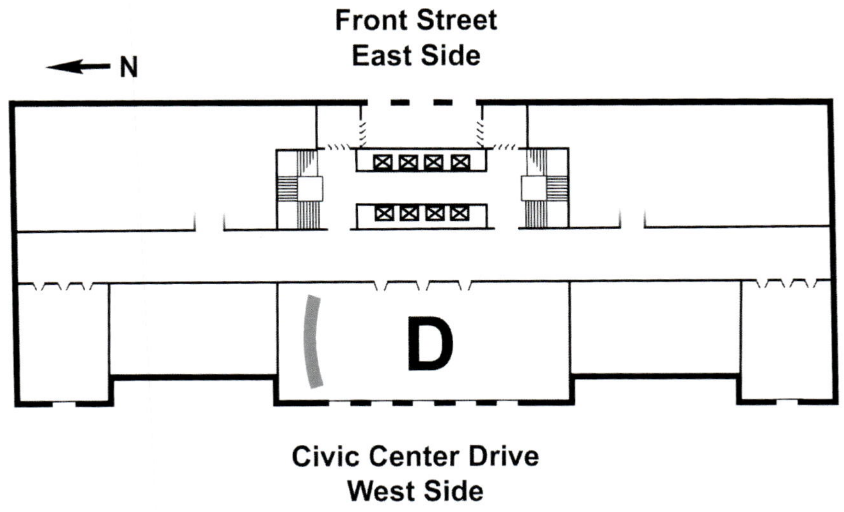

Fig. 6–1. The first-floor plan of the Ohio Judicial Center. *D,* In the Supreme Courtroom, note the new bench, shown as a curved bar at the north end. Also shown are three doors to the grand concourse and five windows to the west side exterior.

Fig. 6-2. Looking toward the bench (north end) of the Supreme Courtroom. The doors from the grand concourse are on the right, and the windows to the west are on the left.

For this room, the architect, Hake, chose the impressive character of the older Beaux Arts style. We might expect that the decoration of the room was changed during the renovation to the Supreme Courtroom from 2001 to 2004, but the only changes were the addition of a new Supreme Court bench and the decorative dividers separating seating sections of the room.

On the south end of the Supreme Courtroom (FIG. 6-3), a long mural extends across the south wall of the room just below the ceiling from the east to west wall. This painting is in a more traditional Beaux Arts style, with the expected breadth and containing many small figures. Around the courtroom are fourteen smaller murals that depict important scenes from Ohio and American history.

Rudolf Scheffler (see p. 47) painted all the murals in the Supreme Courtroom. The mural style here is not the grand Beaux Arts style; rather, these large murals are filled with two or three human figures depicted close together. Each mural has the year in history noted on the frame; the title of each mural is listed in the construction documents. The paintings start with 1749 on the south end of the west wall and progress around the room to the north, ending with 1863 on the south end of the east wall, and each bears an inscription.

Fig. 6-3. The south end of the Supreme Courtroom. The windows to the west are on the right, and the doors from the grand concourse are on the left.

"1749: Céleron de Bienville takes possession for France of the territory now known as Ohio, burying leaden tablets in the Ohio River" (Fig. 6–4*A*)

In 1749, Pierre-Joseph Céleron de Bienville, a Frenchman, was sent by the governor of New France, in Quebec, to the Ohio Territory to claim it for France. The mural shows two French soldiers burying tablets inscribed with "1749" and "Louis the 15th King of France."

"1750: Christopher Gist builds forts along the Ohio and Scioto Rivers for the British" (Fig. 6–4*B*)

In 1750, the British explorer and surveyor Christopher Gist was hired by the Ohio Company of Virginia to find a site in the Northwest Territory for a new land settlement. Gist was not well received by the French already in the area. The record does not verify that Gist's expedition constructed forts, in spite of the mural showing this activity.

"1755: Braddock's Retreat" (Fig. 6–4*C*)

In 1755, during the French and Indian War, British General Edward Braddock took a force of 2,000 British troops to capture the French Fort Duquesne

A B C

Fig. 6-4. Murals on the walls of the Supreme Courtroom, starting on the west wall at the south end. *A*, "1749: Céleron de Bienville"; *B*, "1750: Christopher Gist builds forts along the Ohio and Scioto Rivers for the British"; *C*, "1755: Braddock's Retreat."

(now Pittsburgh). However, the French, with American Indian allies, severely defeated Braddock's troops in a surprise attack on July 9, 1755. The British lost more than half of their soldiers, and General Braddock was injured and died shortly afterwards.

"1749–1755: Washington Raising the British Flag at Fort Duquesne" (Fig. 6–5*A*)

In the fall of 1758, a much younger George Washington than shown in the mural was a member of the British Colonial First Virginia Regiment, part of an expedition under British General John Forbes sent to capture Fort Duquesne from the French. Forbes planned a major attack, but the night before, the French had abandoned the fort and set it on fire. The next day, George Washington raised the British flag over what was left of the badly burned Fort Duquesne, which looked very different from the intact fort shown in the mural. The source of the dates on this mural is unknown and does not agree with other sources, which list the events as occurring during 1758.

"1764: Treaty with Pontiac" (Fig. 6–5*B*)

As a result of the British treaty that ended the French and Indian War, the American Indians' hopes of an independent land in America vanished. American Indians' rebellion against the British was known as Pontiac's War. Ottawa Chief Pontiac led American Indians in attacks on British forts, capturing Fort Sandusky, Fort Detroit, and Fort Pitt. Starting in 1763, a series of treaties was negotiated between the British and the rebelling tribes, finally ending the hostilities with a treaty in 1766.

A B C

Fig. 6-5. Murals on the walls of the Supreme Courtroom, starting on the west wall in the middle and ending at the north. *A*, "1749–1755: Washington Raising the British Flag at Fort Duquesne"; *B*, "1764: Treaty with Pontiac"; *C*, "1788–1794: Manasseh Cutler."

"1788–1794: Manasseh Cutler Plans the Establishment of Schools and Churches in Ohio" (Fig. 6–5*C*)

Reverend Manasseh Cutler worked with the Congress of the Confederation, and was instrumental in enacting the Northwest Ordinance of 1787, which established the government of the Northwest Territory. From Congress, Cutler obtained over a million acres in southeastern Ohio for the Boston-based Ohio Company of Associates, land that he helped develop into Marietta, the first town in the Northwest Territory.

"1794: The Battle of Fallen Timbers" (Fig. 6–6*A*)

American Indians were expecting a land of their own after the Revolutionary War, but that did not happen. Following two victories by an American Indian confederation over American soldiers, President Washington gave command of the American soldiers to General Anthony Wayne. On August 20, 1794, American soldiers met the American Indian confederation, led by Shawnee Chief Blue Jacket, at an area known as Fallen Timbers. The confederation of American Indians was badly beaten, which put an end to organized American Indian resistance in the Northwest Territories.

"1796: The Evacuation of Detroit" (Fig. 6–6*B*)

Years after the end of the Revolutionary War, the Jay Treaty of 1794 between the United States and Britain declared, among other things, that British troops were to surrender all posts in America, including Fort Detroit. The American troops under Captain Moses Porter on July 7, 1796, watched the British lower their Union Jack and evacuate the fort, and Captain Moses then raised Old Glory over the fort. This mural depicts a minor event in American history that was not part of Ohio history.

A B C

Fig. 6-6. Murals on the walls of the Supreme Courtroom across the north end and on the east wall at the north end. *A*, "1794: The Battle of Fallen Timbers"; *B*, "1796: The Evacuation of Detroit"; *C*, "1813: The Death of Tecumseh."

"1813: The Death of Tecumseh" (Fig. 6–6*C*)

In the War of 1812, Shawnee leader Tecumseh sided with the British against the Americans in an attempt to remove the Americans from ancestral American Indian land in the Northwest Territory. American General William Henry Harrison led a large army that chased the retreating British troops and the American Indian confederacy into Canada along the Thames River, near Moraviantown, Ontario. Harrison's troops engaged British troops and American Indian fighters in the final battle, where Tecumseh was killed, on October 5, 1813.

"1813: Commodore Perry's Victory on Lake Erie" (Fig. 6–7*A*)

The War of 1812 was going poorly for America, with multiple victories for the British. American Commodore Oliver Hazard Perry engaged the British Navy in the Battle of Lake Erie on September 10, 1813. Perry's maneuvering proved decisive, and the British surrendered at midafternoon. Perry sent a dispatch to General Harrison reading, "We have met the enemy and they are ours."

"1816: Establishment of the State Government at Columbus, Ohio" (Fig. 6–7*B*)

Following the War of 1812, the political power in the State of Ohio moved to the center of the state. A new town, Columbus, was named and plotted on a bluff over the Scioto River across from Franklinton, Ohio. Columbus received its city charter in 1816. Later that same year, the Ohio state capital was moved to Columbus from Chillicothe.

"1832: Opening of the Ohio-Erie Canal" (Fig. 6–7*C*)

In 1822, the Ohio Board of Canal Commissioners was established to build

Above: **Fig. 6-7.** Murals on the walls of the Supreme Courtroom on the east wall between the doors. *A,* "1813: Commodore Perry's Victory on Lake Erie"; *B,* "1816: Establishment of the state government at Columbus, Ohio"; *C,* "1832: Opening of the Ohio-Erie Canal."

Left: **Fig. 6-8.** Murals on the walls of the Supreme Courtroom on the south end of the east wall. *A,* "1841: Departure of the last American Indians for the reservations"; *B,* "1863: Defeat of the Confederate cavalry and General John Morgan at Buffington, West Virginia."

a series of canals for carrying goods and people. With the rivers in the north of Ohio flowing to Lake Erie and the rivers in the south flowing to the Ohio River, there was a need for north-south cross-state transportation that was both cheap and fast. The title of this mural refers to the Erie Canal opening in 1832, but the men in the mural are shown breaking ground with hand shovels as they would have at the beginning of construction in 1825.

"1841: Departure of the Last American Indians for the Reservations" (Fig. 6–8*A*)

The US Congress passed the Indian Removal Act of 1830, which was signed by President Andrew Jackson. This act forced southern tribes east of the Mississippi River to move to lands west of the Mississippi River, and it

Fig. 6–9. Mural on the south wall of the Supreme Courtroom.

forced the relocation of Ohio tribes that had previously signed treaties to retain their small reservation. But after much government pressure, these tribes finally moved west of the Mississippi River to get more land and to preserve their culture. The Ohio tribes departed slowly, beginning with the Seneca in 1831, then the Shawnee and the Ottawa in 1832, and the Wyandot in 1837. The forced relocation of American Indian tribes in the south became known as the Trail of Tears, a term that also applies to the Ohio tribes. The mural shows a settler indicating that American Indians must leave Ohio. In the 1930s, this event was viewed as important enough that it should be prominently displayed as a part of Ohio history.

"1863: Defeat of the Confederate Cavalry and General John Morgan at Buffington, West Virginia" (Fig. 6–8*B*)

During the Civil War, the Ohio River served as a division between the Union and the Southern Confederacy. In July of 1863, Confederate General John Hunt Morgan crossed into Ohio near Cincinnati. Moving eastward, he attacked Union forts and towns north of the Ohio River, with Union troops chasing Morgan to the east as he tried to escape into West Virginia at Buffington Island in the Ohio River. With the help of Union warships in the Ohio River to block the exit route, Union forces were able to capture the Confederate troops.

Finally, the majestic panorama at the south end of the courtroom (FIG. 6–9), dated 1788, offers a composite of many scenes. The following description is based on the construction documents. In the background, there is a view from a bluff overlooking Marietta, Ohio, with the land office of the Ohio Company in the center. The mural has thirteen figures, including children, representing the original thirteen states.

From the left, Miami leader Little Turtle stands under the trees with an American Indian girl near him. In the next group is a standing settler proudly holding a string of fish representing the abundance of nature in Ohio. Leaning on a pile of books is the Reverend Manasseh Cutler, symbolizing his role in establishing the Ohio Territory and his interest in education. In the center stands General Rufus Putnam, a founder of the Ohio Company of Associates, and General Arthur St. Clair, governor of the Northwest Territory. A boy holds General St. Clair's horse. To the right are a woman working on corn and a girl with a dead deer. Next are three men working as wheelwrights and one man pointing to the center, indicating progress from the past. The last person on the right is a scout often mentioned in folklore, listed here as Issac Hunter, dressed in buckskins and holding his long rifle.

At least three of Scheffler's murals include images copied from earlier works created by other artists. The painting of Braddock's defeat is based on an original engraving published by Alonzo Chappel in *Life and Times of Washington,* volume 1, in 1857 (FIG. 6–10), though only the center was used (FIG. 6–11). The composition of the painting of Tecumseh's death was published by Philip Banks as en engraving in 1813. Scheffler's painting includes the lower left area of the engraving. The painting of George Washington before the Revolutionary War raising the British flag at Fort Duquesne is from a larger original image drawn and engraved by John R. Chapin and T. B. Smith, found in an 1859 book by John Lossing.

Scheffler's work in the Supreme Courtroom reflects the extent of his education in American history, having moved to the United States at the age of 40 from Germany. Painting murals of Ohio history after being in the US for only seven years was no doubt a challenge. After receiving the commission in 1931, he looked in books and encyclopedias for help in selecting and

Fig. 6-10. Original engraving of Braddock's defeat from 1857.

deciding how to paint specific events. Research by historian Stuart Hobbs confirms that Scheffler used an encyclopedia to select the topics for the murals. Another influence could have been Scheffler's life in Germany in the early 1900s. At that time, there was an avid interest among Germans in idealized Americana. In addition to translations of John Fenimore Cooper's books into German, the works authored by the German Karl May romanticized the American West. Scheffler's approach to his historic murals likely took this perspective.

It is notable that the American Indians included in many of the wall murals were depicted as brave fighting men, even though they always ultimately lost to the settlers and soldiers. American Indians were inaccurately portrayed as an aggressive people, without an understanding of their feelings about the loss of their land and their culture.

In thinking about the choice of scenes for these paintings from Ohio history, it is helpful to remember that in the 1930s there was a sense of pride in America's ability to conquer, and a shared belief that strength came from military and physical power. At that time, an understanding of American cultural diversity and its origin was not considered important in mainstream society. Now, almost a hundred years later, historians would probably pick different scenes in Ohio's history to represent key elements and significant persons or groups.

Fig. 6-11. Scheffler's mural from 1932 of Braddock's defeat, in the Supreme Courtroom.

SUPREME COURTROOM: NORTHWEST TERRITORY

The Northwest Territory was the first geographical subdivision of America west of the Appalachian Mountains, and the future home for five states, including Ohio. In the Supreme Courtroom (FIG. 7-1D), the murals on the ceiling depict the five states: Indiana, Ohio, Michigan, Illinois, and Wisconsin. These sections of the mural-rich ceiling are similar to those discussed in the previous chapter, with the mythical deities clothed only in flowing scarves typical of the high regard for classical Greek and Roman forms of the Beaux Arts style. Deep coffers separate the murals and include

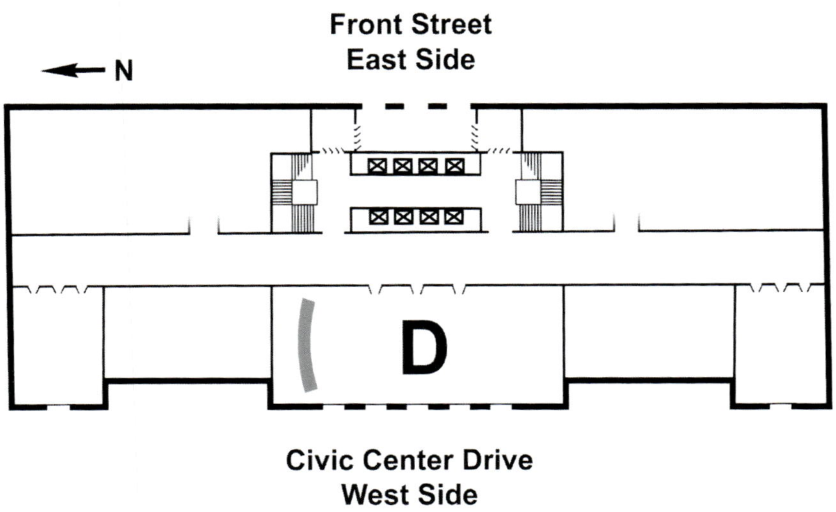

Fig. 7-1. The first floor of the Ohio Judicial Center: *D.* Depicted in the Supreme Courtroom is a new bench in gray (curved line) at the north end. Also shown are three doors to the grand concourse and five windows to the west side exterior.

Fig. 7-2. The ceiling of the Supreme Courtroom, with the mural representing Ohio near the bottom and that of Michigan at the top, showing the detail and depth of the coffers containing recessed murals.

detailed plaster features painted with gold leaf (FIG. 7–2). The minute detail of relief and color on the coffers required hours of work for painting and is reminiscent of Baroque borders seen in Europe. In other American buildings of the time, ceiling murals were commonly edged with a small plaster rim, or even a shallow decorative border, to separate them. The deep, complex coffers separating the ceiling murals at the Ohio Judicial Center are a remarkable sight. The richness in the ceiling's gilding, the detailed relief of the plaster coffers, and the sheer number of murals are unique among ceilings constructed during that time. Including the five murals of the states formerly in the Northwest Territory, there are a total of 33 individual murals on the ceiling (FIG. 7–3). The artist responsible for the murals was Rudolf Scheffler (see p. 47).

The center murals for each state contain an outline map and mythological figures that allude to the industrial capabilities and products of the state. Fortunately, the building documents supply a description of these murals.

Fig. 7-3. The entire ceiling of the Supreme Courtroom, with south to the top, north to the bottom, east to the right, and west to the left.

A

B

Fig. 7-4. Ceiling murals from the Supreme Courtroom, with states formerly of the Northwest Territory represented. *A*, "Wisconsin"; *B*, "Michigan."

At the south end of the ceiling (FIG. 7–4A), Wisconsin is light pink, and Lake Michigan to the right is pale blue. The panel features a young American Indian woman riding a bull, representing Pomona, the Roman goddess of fruitful abundance, as a symbol of the productivity of Wisconsin. Industry is symbolized by the man at the lower left seated on a ram's skin with a spindle of wool.

Michigan (FIG. 7–4B) is shown in red, including the Upper Peninsula. In the center, an American Indian from the Algonquin tribe reclines on a bison skin with a cluster of arrows in his right hand. The significance of this is not explained in the architectural documents. An industry of key importance, lumber, is indicated by the man sitting in a tree with a hatchet. The central importance of pottery is shown by a woman on the left surrounded by clay pots. The importance of food production is highlighted on the right with a woman holding an apple and a man sitting in a fishing boat.

Ohio (FIG. 7–5A) is pink with a pale blue Lake Erie at the top, and the surrounding states are dark red. In the center is Mercury, who holds a wild horse in one hand and his staff in the other. The horse represents the energetic Ohio Company of Associates that opened Ohio for settlers at Marietta, Ohio. Oil production and agriculture are symbolized on the left with an oil lamp, a sheaf of grain, and a horse plow. Emphasizing Ohio agriculture on the right are a scythe and bundles of grain.

Illinois (FIG. 7–5B) is red, and its surrounding states are pink. Hercules, the Roman god, has his hand on a hammer and anvil next to a wagon wheel, emphasizing the role of industry in the state. On the left below is a woman raking grain, to demonstrate the importance of agriculture. The man in a tree evokes the role of lumbering in the Illinois economy. The woman below with a loom containing an American Indian pattern emphasizes the importance of the textile industry.

Indiana (FIG. 7–6) is presented in pink, and the surrounding states in red. Over the state is the floating figure of Flora, the Roman goddess of flowers and spring, with a cherub carrying a torch and riding on her back to demonstrate the learned youth of the state. Below Flora is a cherub picking the

A

B

Fig. 7–5. Ceiling murals from the Supreme Courtroom, with states formerly of the Northwest Territory represented. *A*, "Ohio"; *B*, "Illinois."

Fig. 7–6. Ceiling mural from the Supreme Courtroom, with Indiana represented as one of the states formerly of the Northwest Territory.

leaves of tobacco growing in Kentucky, which at the time was processed in Indiana. The three women flying from the east represent commerce in the fields of agriculture, industry, and chemistry. The man below on the right with a caliper compass and a circular piece of metal represents engineering and industry. On the left are men working on a steel girder for a building, to symbolize construction.

The five murals of the states show the strengths of each state, with few differences among them. American Indians appear in all the murals except the one of Indiana, and their role seems to be to support the state economy. These images of American Indians represent a romanticized view and do not represent the political reality of the treatment of American Indians. Otherwise, while the murals are interesting, the imagery and symbolism are straightforward.

In the corners of the courtroom ceiling are the state seals of the four states found in the former Northwest Territory, excluding Ohio (FIG. 7–7). These are highly stylized versions of the state seals, with little detail and no words. Each mural has a man and a woman who are variously resting next to the seal or have brushes in their hands as if they were working on the seals.

The Wisconsin state seal in the southwest corner represents a historic version from 1875 (FIG. 7–7A). The state animal, the badger, is at the top, and on one side are standing a cowboy holding a rope and a workman holding a pick. The shield bears the US coat of arms and a crossed pick and shovel.

The Michigan state seal, displayed in the southeast corner, is different from all official versions but includes many of the same elements (FIG. 7–7B). The eagle at the top is a symbol of the United States. An elk on the left and a moose on the right each hold a shield with their front legs, and water surrounds a peninsula of land. A man with a rifle in his left hand symbolizes readiness to defend the nation.

The seal of the State of Indiana is found in the northwest corner of the courtroom ceiling (FIG. 7–7C). It shows a buffalo jumping over a log and a woodsman cutting down two sycamore trees.

The Illinois state seal shown in the northeast corner features a bald eagle on a rock carrying a shield with thirteen stars representing the original states of the Union (FIG. 7–7D). This version was used when Illinois was part of the Northwest Territory and was then changed to the current seal. The eagle is carrying a banner that cannot be read here, but the official seal reads, "State Sovereignty, National Union."

The painted seal of Ohio is centered at the north end of the courtroom over the Supreme Court Bench and above the red curtain (FIG. 7–8). This

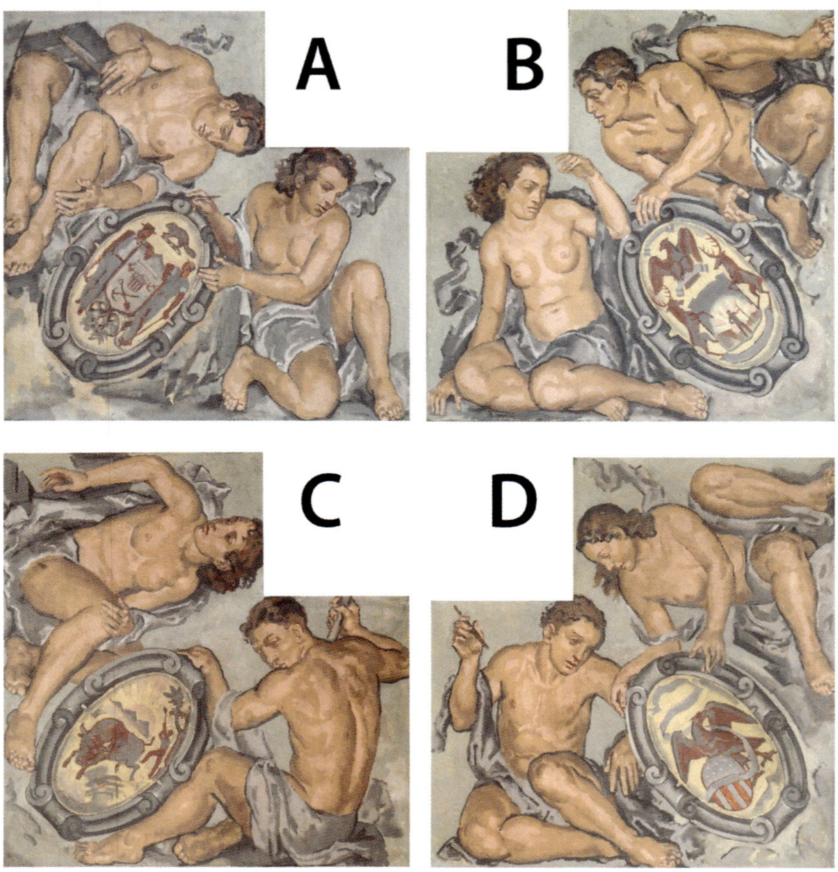

Fig. 7–7. On the ceiling of the Supreme Courtroom at the four corners are four state seals. *A,* Wisconsin, southwest corner; *B,* Michigan, southeast corner; *C,* Indiana, northwest corner; *D,* Illinois, northeast corner.

Fig. 7-8. The stylized Ohio state seal at the center of the north end of the ceiling of the Supreme Courtroom.

is a highly stylized version, with balances of justice added to it, despite that no one at that time knew that the room would become a Supreme Courtroom.

Smaller murals at the sides of the Supreme Courtroom ceiling show human figures dressed in Roman garb, representing eight important activities carried out in the five states formerly of the Northwest Territory (FIG. 7–9). The activities are listed in the architect's documents, but the position in the ceiling for each activity's mural is not indicated. "Agriculture" (FIG. 7–9A) has a cornucopia, bundle of wheat, and garland of flowers. "Engineering" (FIG. 7–9B) shows a man holding the girder of a building, with a milling machine and canon nearby. "Education" (FIG. 7–9C) displays books and an owl in the lower corner. "Mining" (FIG. 7–9D) is an image of a man underground chipping at a wall. "Science" (FIG. 7–9E) is shown with machines. "Surveying" (FIG. 7–9F) has books and stones with writing but does not easily fit any of the panels; it was assigned here as the only title not used elsewhere. "Industry" (FIG. 7–9G) has a man in a toga with a plumb bob in his hand, flanked by scenes of factory smokestacks and a field of oil fields. "Technique" (FIG. 7–9H), with a painter's palate and drawing instruments, was at that time associated with performing arts, but in recent times the term is more widely associated with science. Note that the contents of panels assigned to "Science" (FIG. 8–9E) and "Engineering" (FIG. 8–9B) could be reversed.

Next, on either side of the five states are ten small rectangular octagon panels, symbolizing industry and commerce (FIG. 7–3). The specified names

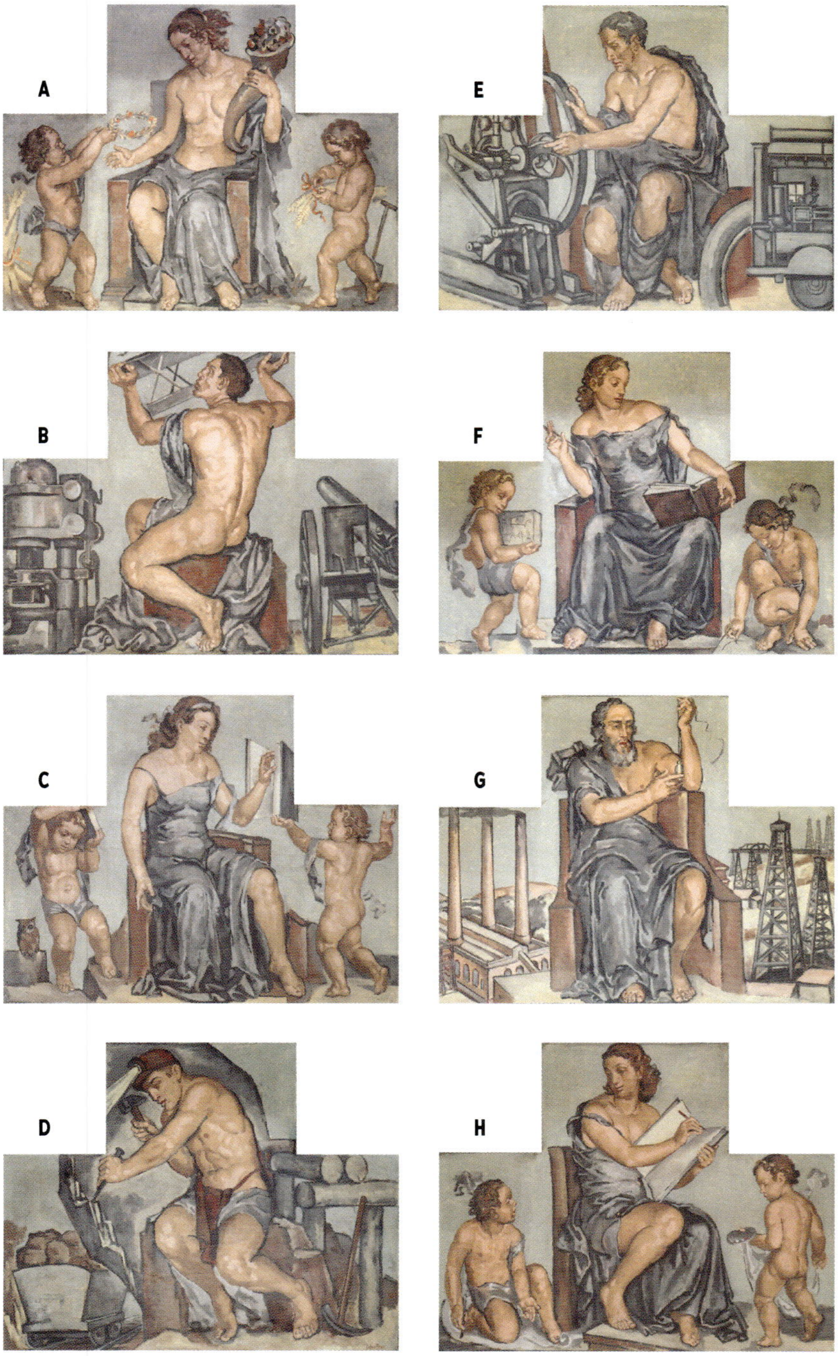

Fig. 7–9. Murals from the sides of the Supreme Courtroom ceiling, beginning with *A* to *D* on the west side at the south end and *E* to *H* on the east side starting at the south. The eight important activities carried out in the states formerly of the Northwest Territory. *A*, "Agriculture"; *B*, "Engineering"; *C*, "Education"; *D*, "Mining"; *E*, "Science"; *F*, "Surveying"; *G*, "Industry"; *H*, "Technique."

for these murals in the architectural drawings are different from those of the images in the murals. The original titles of the ten small landscapes were "Can Factory," "Oil Field," "Hay Harvest," "Logging," "Riverboats on the Ohio River," "Ohio River Lock," "Clay Mountains on Lake Michigan," "Fishing," "Devils Door in Wisconsin," and "Lonely Rock in Northern Wisconsin." The final images in the panels and the titles later assigned to them do a better job than the original list of describing the industries of these five states. For example, in a panel representing communication (FIG. 7–10*H*), the extinct carrier pigeon is shown. However, the title of "Education" (FIG. 7–10*C*) does

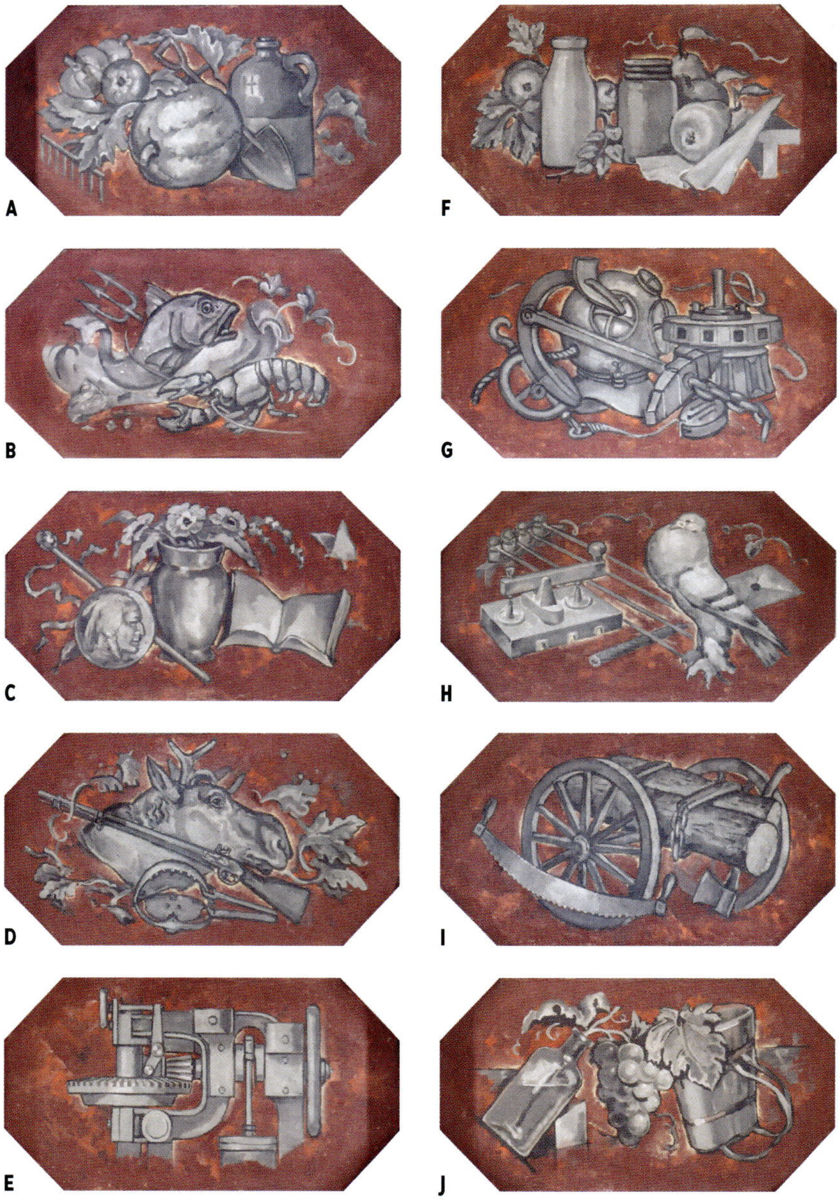

Fig. 7–10. Ten murals on the Supreme Courtroom ceiling on either side of the panels representing the industry and commerce of the five states located in the former Northwest Territories. Starting at the south end, with panels *A* to *E* on the west side and panels *F* to *J* on the east side. New titles have been assigned by the author based on what is actually presented in the panels. *A*, "Farming"; *B*, "Fishing"; *C*, "Education"; *D*, "Hunting"; *E*, "Engineering"; *F*, "Canning"; *G*, "Seafaring"; *H*, "Communication"; *I*, "Logging"; *J*, "Viniculture."

not easily fit the objects shown in the corresponding image, and the title that Scheffler had in mind is not known. It would be interesting to know how Scheffler arrived at the final topics for the murals and who recommended the original titles.

The final series of six rectangular murals down the center of the ceiling represents the fruits and other produce of the five states; there were no titles for these murals in the construction documents (FIG. 7–11). Each of these panels shows a flower arrangement that Scheffler chose to paint in gray tones, rather than colors as might be expected.

The overall impression created by the Supreme Courtroom ceiling is that of a spectacular collection of artworks, with its numerous murals and deep coffers decorated with intricate designs covered in colors and gold leaf. After studying the murals, it becomes clear that the murals contain much more detail than is suggested in their titles. This room is truly a fine example of Beaux-Arts architecture, constructed in a way that has never

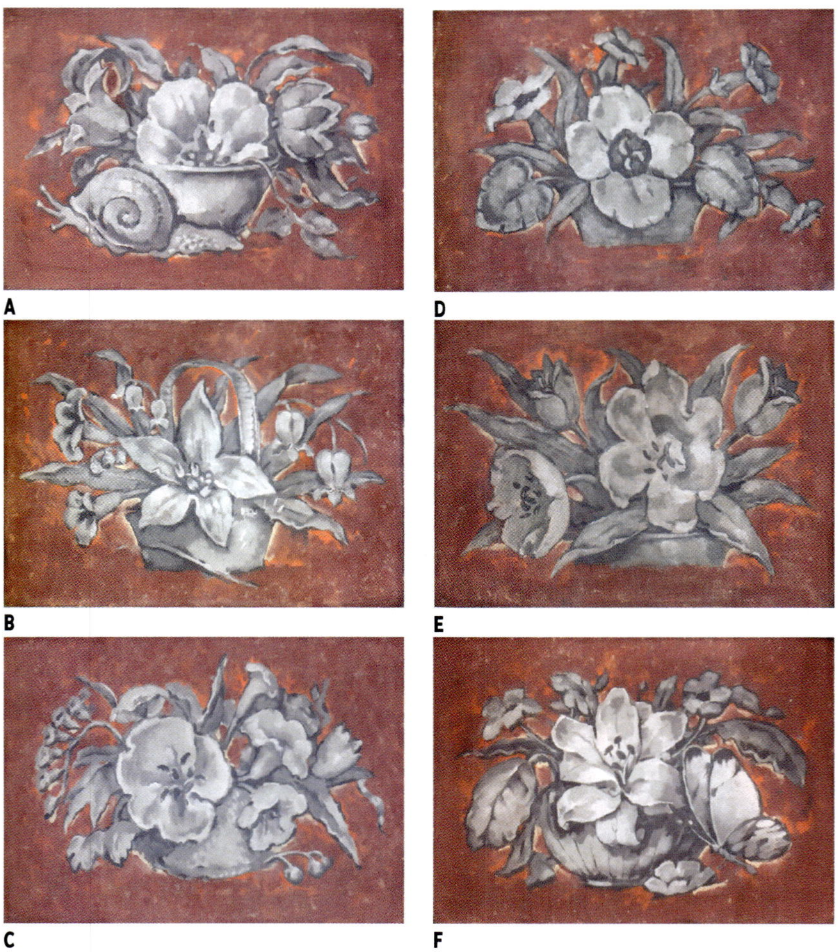

Fig. 7–11. Six murals in the Supreme Courtroom ceiling centered between the murals representing the fruits and products for the five states located in the former Northwest Territories: Panel *A* is on the south end, and panel *F* is on the north end.

been repeated. While there is controversy about the meaning and importance of some murals, they represent the art of 1933 very effectively.

From a historical perspective, the selection of the subjects for the murals in this room is important. Did Harry Hake select the titles of the art, or did Wiley or Scheffler? It is likely that Scheffler suggested images and Wiley approved them. How likely is it that Scheffler changed the images after the preliminary sketches were approved and thus exercised his "artistic license"? We will never know.

OHIO'S PAST AND PRESENT

On the first floor of the Ohio Judicial Center, located at opposite ends, there are two small hearing rooms of similar size and shape (FIG. 8–1E and F). Both rooms incorporate murals telling the story of Ohio's industrial development. These murals depict both early commerce as well as 1930s-era industry. In 1840s Ohio, commerce consisted of such handmade household items as clothes and tools. Construction was of wood, with boards hand-cut from local trees. Agriculture was food grown on nearby farms and sold by the farmer. Industry in 1933 was proudly shown in juxtaposition, with tall

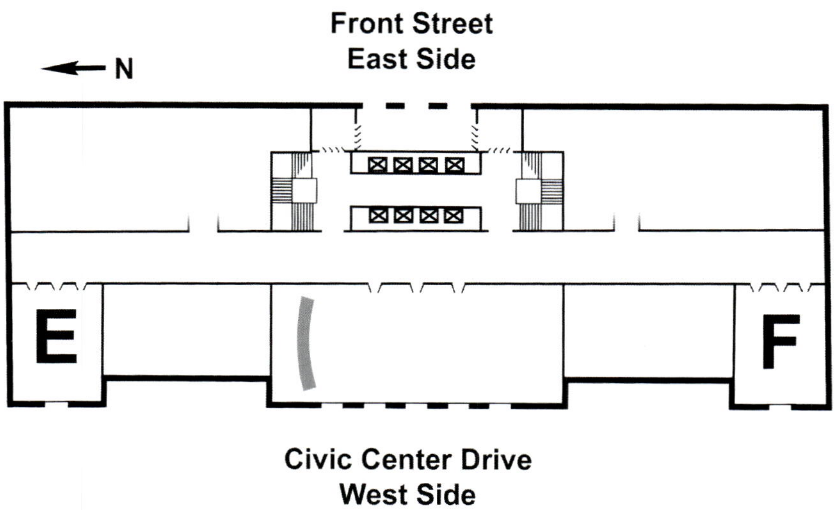

Fig. 8–1. The first-floor plan of the Ohio Judicial Center. *E*, north hearing room 106; *F*, south hearing room 102.

billowing smokestacks, trains, canals, automobiles, and propeller airplanes. Industrial work in 1933 was powered by an electric motor or gas engine, widely accepted as a huge improvement over working by hand and requiring many laborers to complete the same amount of work. While from the standpoint of the present this level of progress might not seem like enough to celebrate, in 1933 people were proud of the new industrial age and all of the potential it had brought. Examining the modern industry of 1933 gives us a historical picture of Ohio almost a hundred years ago.

Hearing room 106, the north room (FIG. 8–1E), was used in the 1930s by the Industrial Commission of Ohio. The theme of the room's murals is given as "Progress of Industry." The murals on the walls possess the range of colors, textures, and shapes typical of 1930s Art Deco style (FIG. 8–2). A band of decorative art encircles the room just below the ceiling, also in typical Art Deco style, and includes circular and rectangular reliefs with patterns of flowers and leaves (FIG. 8–3). These eleven vivid murals are the creation of John Holmer (1894–1962), who was educated in and lived in Cincinnati, Ohio. Holmer attended the Art Academy of Cincinnati and

Fig. 8-2. North hearing room 106, looking west at the window covered by red drapes. The large mural on the right or north shows images of early Ohio commerce, and the mural on the left or south wall depicts 1933 commerce.

A B C

studied art in Paris and Rome. He worked as a mural painter in the decorating business, and he painted numerous easel paintings.

Surrounding the room is a sequence of scenes from early to 1930s-era Ohio. On the north wall are murals containing scenes of early Ohio industry and agriculture (FIG. 8–4). Holmer tied these three sets of panels together by including a river at the top of each. The narrow left mural depicts early industry in the form of pottery production (FIG. 8–4A). The large middle mural shows a farmyard in operation near a small log house (FIG. 8–4B). The narrow right mural shows a construction project, probably a house (FIG. 8–4C).

Holmer used solid colors with a lack of detail to give a smooth simple texture to his Art Deco murals. The center mural demonstrates this style in depicting farm fields, shown in a single color with no texture to indicate plants leaves; similarly, the cut wood is shown in solid colors with no grain markings.

On the east wall, above the three entrance doors to hearing room 106 (FIG. 8–5), are three short panels that Holmer used to connect the motifs

Top: Fig. 8-3. Plaster relief designs near the ceiling in north hearing room 106.

Above: Fig. 8-4. Hearing room 106, north wall murals of Ohio's past commerce, with large central mural depicting a farm (*B*), and elongated, narrow side murals have the industry of pottery on the west (left, *A*) and construction on the east (right, *C*).

of early work on the north wall and modern, 1930s-era work on the south wall. The north panel shows several Conestoga wagons with settlers arriving in Ohio (FIG. 8–5A). The small center panel shows a rural landscape, with roofs of houses, a church steeple, and farmland with a river behind it (FIG. 8–5B). The right panel completes the historic progression, showing 1930s factories with smokestacks and, in the distance, oil derricks (FIG. 8–5C). Men are depicted working with machines in a factory, and below them are railroad cars loaded with coal. Holmer used a river flowing through all three murals at the top to unite the different time periods, showing the continuity of growth from early settlers to modern industrial production. In the right and left mural are ventilation grills in the Art Deco style. In the middle mural is a working clockface with Roman numerals.

Covering the south wall of hearing room 106 are scenes of 1930s industry (FIG. 8–6). These scenes show the great new power of machines in building a modern 1930s city in Ohio. The narrow left panel portrays a factory where building beams are being machined (FIG. 8–6A). The large center panel has a city with skyscrapers on the distant side of the river in the background (FIG. 8–6B). On the near side of the river, exciting symbols of progress are seen, with many smokestacks, grain silos, and trains. Men

Fig. 8–5. The east wall of hearing room 106, with murals above the three doors, the north (left, *A*), middle (*B*), and south (left, *C*). These murals depict a transition from Ohio's past (*A*) to its present in 1933 (*C*).

A

B

C

at the bottom right heat bolts to place in the holes of the beams. Although nearly all skilled workers in the 1930s were white men, Holmer did include one Black man, who uses a wheelbarrow in the lower right of the center mural. From today's perspective, it is surprising that in all of the building's murals there is only one Black man, especially considering that Ohio was a major abolitionist state during the Civil War and a prominent state in the Underground Railroad. The narrow panel to the right focuses on stone cutting for use in building (FIG. 8–6C).

At the west end of the room, there are two narrow murals (FIG. 8–7) on either side of a draped center window (FIG. 8–2). As with the east murals, these paintings illustrate a transition from modern work to early labor and the farm. The left narrow panel is a factory that makes large machines (FIG. 8–7A). The right narrow panel depicts a blacksmith shop of earlier times (FIG. 8–7B).

Offering a different view of Ohio past and present, the murals in hearing room 102, on the south end of the building (FIG. 8–1F), use Ohio maps to tell the story of commerce and transportation (FIG. 8–8). These murals, painted in a traditional style, contain a great deal of detail and many small figures. In spite of the huge murals being two-dimensional, the small figures create additional perspective and help to convey the power of commerce in Ohio. While people and objects are painted in different scales

Fig. 8–6. Murals on the south wall in hearing room 106 depict what was Ohio's present in 1933 with a large central mural (*B*) and elongated side murals: *A* to the east and *C* to the west.

A

B

C

A

B

and sometimes from different points of view, they fit together perfectly, frequently with humor. Above the murals is an ornament decorating the band of plaster reliefs encircling the room just below the ceiling, and the large image in the rectangle is of bird wings with a symbol of a propeller at the center (FIG. 8–9).

In this room, the six murals (FIGS. 8–10 and 8–11) were painted by Herman H. Wessel (1878–1969), who was born in Indiana to Prussian immigrant parents. In 1896, he enrolled in the Art Academy of Cincinnati, later spending three years in Munich and Paris studying painting. Upon his return to Cincinnati, he took a job teaching at the Art Academy, where he remained until his retirement in 1947.

The center mural on the north wall is a map of Ohio titled *Early Commerce in Ohio* (FIG. 8–10B) and showing the National Road running through Columbus. The map contains a great deal of historic detail, and it is interesting to look at the individual vignettes. For example, at the far right is a Conestoga wagon used by settlers coming west to Ohio on the National Road, which

Facing page: Fig. 8–7. The west window of room 106 features two elongated murals on the south (left, *A*) and the north (right, *B*). These murals show activities that transition backwards from what was the present in 1933 to Ohio's past.

Above: Fig. 8–8. Hearing room 102, looking west, with a center window draped in red. Large murals are visible on the north to the right and south to the left.

A B C

Top: Fig. 8-9. Band of plaster relief at the top of the wall in hearing room 102.

Above: Fig. 8-10. Commerce of Ohio's past is shown in three murals on the north wall of hearing room 102. A large map mural (*B*) with long murals on either side showing a city market (*A*) and an early French trader (*C*).

began in the early 1800s. At the top, to represent water transportation, Lake Erie is shown hosting a large schooner and a side-wheeler paddle wheel, and at the bottom is the Ohio River, with a large stern-wheeler paddleboat at the bottom left. The canal boat on the right represents an important transportation system in the mid-1800s that connected Lake Erie to the Ohio River.

The narrow mural on the left (FIG. 8–10A) is titled "Interior of an Old General Store." People of the mid-1800s purchased a wide variety of goods in such establishments. The narrow mural on the right (FIG. 8–10C) is titled "Indian Trading Station from the 1800s." In the center, a trader is bargaining with an American Indian who is buying goods.

The murals on the opposite or south side of the room depict commerce in the twentieth century (Fig. 8–11). The central mural (FIG. 8–11B) has another large map of the State of Ohio, showing modern (1930s) methods of transportation. In the center of the map is Columbus, and clearly visible

A B C

are the Ohio Statehouse, the LeVeque Tower, and the Ohio Judicial Center. Gone are the canals, and now the Ohio River is seen with a large boat pushing barges filled with goods.

Fig. 8–11. Murals on the south wall depicting modern (1930s) transportation and commerce. A large map (*B*) with side murals depicting warehouse work (*A*) and a vibrant marketplace (*C*).

Trains are shown at the four corners of the state, connecting in Columbus. The newest method of transportation is depicted by two propeller airplanes flying over Ohio (see FIG. INTRO-4, p. xv). This mural includes detail and insights into its era, such as the man holding a flag to stop a truck with farm animals so that men can work on the road.

The narrow mural on the left is a modern (1933) freight terminal where goods are received and then distributed to destinations (FIG. 8–11A). Workers are shown moving individual barrels, boxes, crates, and bags. The narrow mural on the right illustrates a city market, with shoppers on the left side and merchants on the right side (FIG. 8–11C). The shoppers are well-dressed women, one with a baby and another with a dog. The tables appear to hold melons, bananas, cabbages, and flowers.

The small mural on the east wall over the center entrance in hearing room 102 is in the Art Deco style and likely not painted by Wessel (FIG. 8–12). Over the center door reclines the Roman god Mercury, who governs commerce and trade. Below the clock, four female figures stand dressed in Roman robes, each holding a new device that was used in the 1930s for

Fig. 8-12. The east wall, with a single mural over the middle door showing the Roman god Mercury and four human figures with 1933 communication devices.

Facing page: Fig. 8-13. East wall mural above the south and north doors in hearing room 102. The same mural pattern and grill are on the west wall, on either side of the window.

communication. From the left, there are a cord telephone held to the ear with its wire in hand, a radio transmission microphone on a stand with wires over the arm, the United States Postal Service's stamps on envelopes in both hands, and a telegraph key for sending Morse code messages, with wires below. Now, almost 100 years later, use of the then innovative electronic devices from the 1930s is so distant that many people would not recognize them. The style of this mural is very different from the others in the room; the use of stencils on the differently colored shapes suggests that it was probably painted by Rambusch, the decorative painter.

All four of the narrow spaces on the walls above the north and south doors and on the west wall on either side of the window contain similar paintings, used mainly to fill space (FIG. 8-13); these appear to be of the same view from above of a forest, with green trees and mounds of tan earth showing through.

These tree murals were painted on a finer canvas than the rest of Wessel's murals and in a different style, and it would have been unusual for Wessel to leave four potential mural spaces without murals. Thus, these green tree paintings were most likely created by the decorative painter Rambusch. This style of work was common to decorative painters of a century ago.

Both of these two hearing rooms express the same theme comparing Ohio's past (the 1800s) and what was then its present (the 1930s). To viewers of the twenty-first century, the murals of the present day of the 1930s, with their smokestacks, propeller airplanes, and coal-burning trains, portray old-fashioned industrial machines.

THE EVOLUTION OF BOOKS

In 1933, in addition to office space for Ohio's growing state government, the plans for the Ohio Judicial Center included a generous amount of shelf space on the top four floors for a modern library. A century ago, the business of a rapidly growing Ohio generated many documents and reports that needed to be organized for accessible reference. In addition, the State Library of Ohio originally included a large collection of books that were available to citizens and residents. The State Library of Ohio supported smaller libraries in the counties and sometimes served as a source of books for schools and clubs as well as individuals, with the result that many people visited the State Library of Ohio. The only space in the library reserved specifically for public art was in the large reading room.

After the 2004 renovation (see chapter 10, p. 103), the entire library space became the Supreme Court's law library, which contains records and documents for the state's lawyers and the Ohio Supreme Court. The entrance doors are on its south wall, with the center door leading to the elevator lobby. Other doors, at the corners of the room's south side, lead to the stacks. The south wall also has built-in oak bookcases, and above the center door in a carved wood pediment is a depiction of a lamp of knowledge and some owls (FIG. 9–1). The pediments over the side doors each show an open book.

On the south wall are seven murals dealing with the evolution of the printed book (FIG. 9–2), by LeRoy Daniel MacMorris. He studied at the Kansas City Art Institute and the Art Institute of Chicago before serving in

Fig. 9-1. The reading room of the law library on the eleventh floor, looking from the north end towards the south.

World War I. After the war, he studied in Paris, then returned to America to take up a long career as a mural artist. The murals here are one of his earliest commissions.

A detailed description of these murals is given in the construction documents. Four of the murals include quotations in non-English languages from the people depicted. Translations are also included in the construction documents. These several quotations are not precisely what the historical record notes the person as saying, but they are similar. The first panel on the east side depicts an early form of writing, showing characters on a large animal tusk (FIG. 9-2A). Factually, however, the earliest surviving examples of writing appear on bone, clay, or stone, not horns, tusks, or antlers, which were used primarily for statues or jewelry.

The second panel from the east side shows the influence of Egyptian and Assyrian cultures (FIG. 9-2B). A Babylonian king stands holding a stone tablet while a woman writes on papyrus paper in a cuneiform script. At the bottom of the mural is a panel containing three examples of writing from these times, with both the left and right ends in Assyrian cuneiform script that translates as: "I will reveal to thee, O Gilgamesh, the hidden word," and "The decision of the Gods to thee I will declare" (FIG. 9–3). The center is in Egyptian pictographic script, translated as: "I would cause thee to love books better than thy mother. I would cause their beauty to enter into the waters of thy spirit and the working of thy mind. It (the love of knowledge) is better than the holding of any high office." We do not know who selected the text, nor who created the pictographs.

Next in the progression are three human figures depicting the influence of Chinese, Semitic, and Greek cultures (FIG. 9–2C). At the bottom of this panel are three sections, from left to right, in Chinese, Greek, and Hebrew.

Fig. 9–2. Murals depicting the evolution of the book, on the south wall of the reading room, beginning on the east side. *A,* early writing; *B,* the influence of the Egyptians and Assyrians; *C,* Chinese, Semitic, and Greek cultures; *D,* "Let us reveal the wisdom of the ages by the light of truth"; *E,* the impact of the Byzantine, Medieval, and Renaissance periods; *F,* the "Enlightened Age" of the twentieth century (1932); and *G,* the future and the importance of science and industry.

Fig. 9–3. Panel, at the bottom of the mural second from the left , showing the influence of the Egyptians and Assyrians, with Egyptian pictographic script in the middle and cuneiform script on either side.

The Chinese proverb, attributed to Confucius, reads: "If your fields are left untilled your granaries will be empty. If your books are left unread your children will be ignorant. The words of the mouth fly away on the wind, the written word abides." The center is a quotation from Aristotle: "Now, reason, as all would admit, exists for the acquisition of knowledge and seeks ends; the means to which are contained in philosophy; why then should philosophy not be pursued without hesitation." On the right is a quotation from the Book of Habakkuk in the Hebrew Bible: "Write the vision and make it plain upon tables, that he may run that readeth it."

The small middle panel is positioned over the center door (FIG. 9–2D) and displays two cherubs, one writing with a feather quill in a book, "Let us reveal the wisdom of the ages by the light of truth," while the other cherub holds a light.

The panel on the west side of the main door shows three human figures, each from a different time period (FIG. 9–2E). A Byzantine queen has an open vellum scroll, and a woman from the Medieval period is seated with a hand-copied book. The third, from the Renaissance period, is a man operating a manual printing press. At the bottom of this panel are three quotes from the different periods. The quote on the left is in Italian, the one in the middle is in Greek, and the one at the right is in Latin. The left statement is from Petrarch: "Only the poet's pure immortal plan outwits the swift mortality of man." The middle quote is from the Shepherd of Hermas: "First of all, speak evil of no man, neither willingly hear him who speaks evil. For, if in truth, you lend ear to it, you become the accomplice to him who speaks evil." At the right is a quote from Virgil's Eclogues: "Come in the last of the ages, in song Cumaean foretold, now is the world's grand cycle begun once more from of old."

The sixth mural represents the "enlightened age" of the twentieth century, as understood in 1930, with a large commercial printing press in the background on the right (FIG. 9–2F). The figures in this mural, unlike the other murals on this wall, are dressed in 1930s attire. Across the bottom of this panel are aphorisms in French, English, and German. At the left, from the fables of Jean de La Fontaine: "Let fools say knowledge has its price." The center is a quotation from the works of Thomas Carlyle: "In books lies the soul of the whole past time; the articulate audible voice of the past.

When the body and material substance of it has altogether vanished like a dream." At the right is a line from Friedrich von Schiller: "World history is the last judgment."

The westernmost panel is MacMorris's vision of the future, emphasizing the importance of science and industry (FIG. 9–2G). The female figure holds a globe in one hand and a book in the other, representing science and its role in discovery. The male figure reads a book held by the woman, and the power of industry is represented by the man's arm resting on an anvil. Although this panel depicts the future, the people are dressed in Greek and Roman clothes. MacMorris, using his artistic license, portrayed the future as a throwback to the classical period. He apparently did not envision a future including the popularity of blue jeans, handheld electronic devices, and electric cars.

MacMorris's ideas portrayed a classical view of writing and languages, which fit with both Beaux Arts and Art Deco ideas that emulated classical antiquity. Also, his murals can be linked with justice, as writing is an important part of recording the rulings of the judicial system.

10

RENOVATION

By 2001, what was then the Departments of State Building had become outmoded and neglected after almost 70 years of use. Without central air-conditioning or up-to-date wiring, it needed major renovation. The force that drove the Ohio General Assembly to fund the renovation was Ohio Supreme Court Chief Justice Thomas J. Moyer and his vision to move the state judicial system into its own building. Since Ohio achieved statehood in 1803, the Ohio Supreme Court had shared facilities with other state agencies. So, in 2004, the completed renovation converted the building into the Ohio Judicial Center. In 2010, after the Chief Justice's untimely death, the building was renamed, in his honor, the Thomas J. Moyer Ohio Judicial Center.

Fortunately, over the years the building had aged without needing major structural repairs, so the renovation focused on updating existing facilities and converting space to the needs of the judicial system. The new major systems that needed attention were the following: heating and air-conditioning, plumbing, electrical systems, elevators, sprinkler systems for fire protection, wiring for computer communication, energy conservation, building security, and disability access. The Columbus architectural firm of Schooley Caldwell Associates was selected for the renovation, led by Robert D. Loversidge, FAIA. Moody Nolan of Columbus was the associate architectural firm, and Messer Construction managed construction.

Architects faced a problem with improving accessibility to the Front Street three-step entrance without altering the original appearance of the

Fig. 10-1. The Front Street entrance with accessibility ramps added during renovation.

building. The solution was to build ramps to both sides of the entrance in the style of the original design. Architects chose to use white marble that matched the building facade, and metal railing that matched the existing metal tiered lights in front of the building (FIG. 10–1). As a result, the new ramps for accessibility appear as though they were part of the original design of the building.

Another accessibility problem, in the ground floor lobby, had been solved by addition of a ramp. Three steps were needed to get from the Civic Center Drive street level to the elevator lobby. Thus, on the south side of the ground floor lobby, a curved ramp was added (FIG. 10–2). This change was completed years prior to the renovation.

A major consideration of the building's new functions went into converting a generic office building into a judicial building. The most important need was for an Ohio Supreme Courtroom that would have the grandeur appropriate for this judicial body. The obvious place for the Supreme Courtroom was the former main hearing room. This space had the necessary feeling of nobility and respect appropriate to the Ohio judicial system, but it lacked a bench for the justices. The existing bench was for three people in the space at the north end where the red curtain is located. The previous bench from the Rhodes Tower courtroom was unsuitable. So, a new wooden bench was designed by the architect, and a commission for a historic art panel was requested. The artist selected was Craig Vandall Stevens of Sunbury, Ohio. Stevens designs and builds custom furniture, is adept in architectural carving, and has written several books on woodworking. Stevens designed and carved the frieze, an architectural ornament consisting of a horizontal sculptured band, at the top of the bench of the Supreme Court bench (FIG. 10–3).

The commission to Stevens included 12 hand-carved wood reliefs depicting events important in the history of the judicial system in Ohio, and the seal of the Ohio Supreme Court. The style Stevens chose is not Beaux Arts but rather a more organic style inspired by the Arts and Crafts movement. Stevens researched which images would be appropriate to use at the top of the bench and conferred with Chief Justice Moyer and the architects.

Fig. 10-2. The ground floor, looking north from the elevator lobby. The wheelchair access is visible on the left.

Fig. 10-3. The new bench in the Supreme Courtroom on the ground floor.

The panels at the top of the bench commemorate historical events, most of which are easily recognizable, though some may need explanation. The importance of county courthouses (FIG. 10–4B) as centers for justice is exemplified with the Washington County Courthouse, built in 1902 in Marietta, Ohio. The Constitution of the United States was passed in 1787 (FIG. 10–4D). The historical reliance on English common law is shown with open law books (FIG. 10–4G). Early surveys in Ohio formed the basis of a large number of cases decided in the judicial system, as many early legal disputes focused on property rights (FIG. 10–4H). Much of the early surveying was inaccurate, and many owners did not file legal claims to their property, resulting in many cases involving property disputes. In one panel, a Supreme Court justice is shown on horseback, riding circuit to hear cases (FIG. 10–4I), since the Ohio Constitution of 1803 appointed three Supreme Court justices and required them to hold court in each of the 88 counties once a year. Another panel shows the lamp and false-bottom wagon used in the Underground Railroad (FIG. 10–4K), memorializing how the State of Ohio did not allow slavery, which is one reason why many runaway

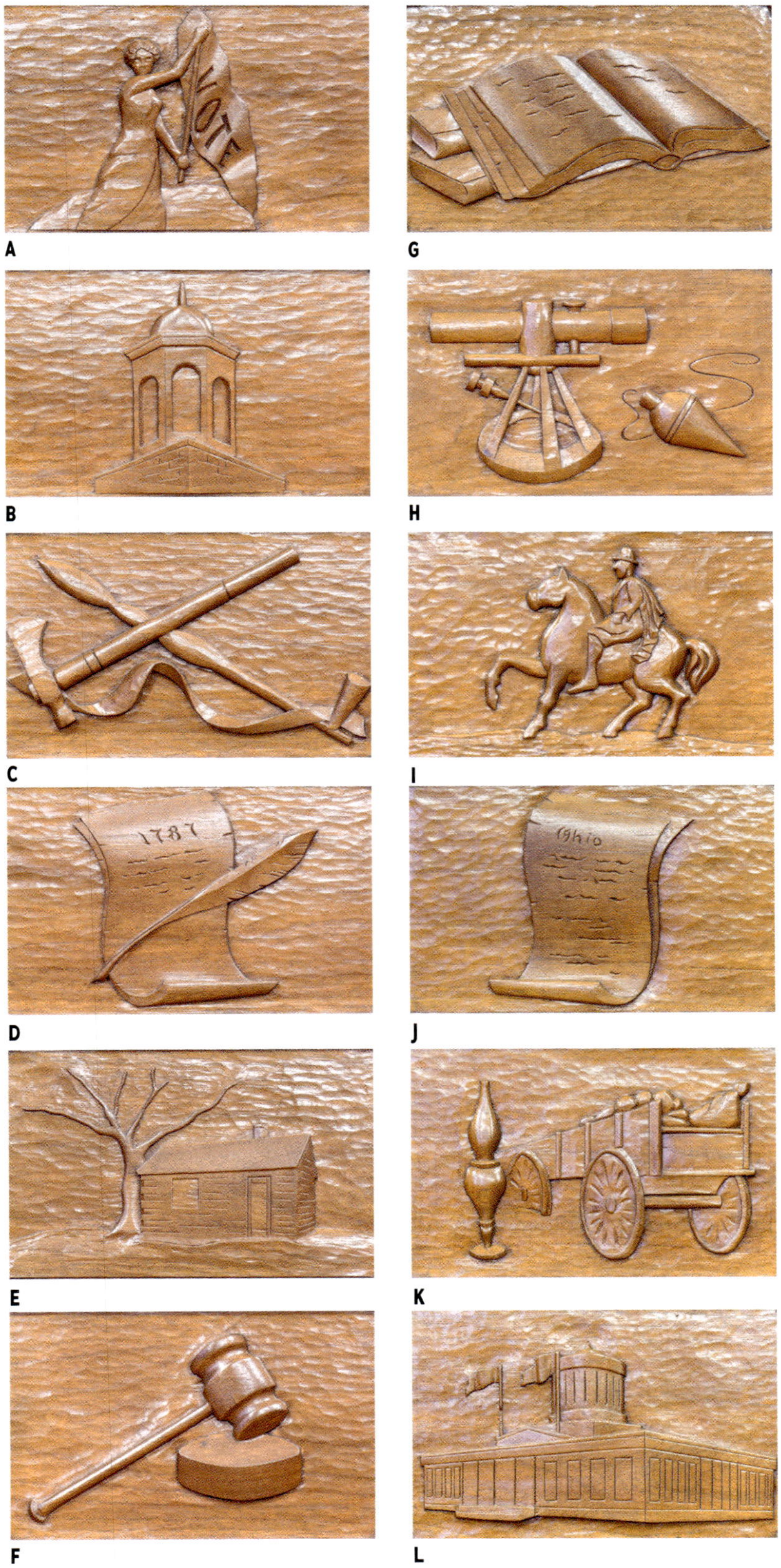

Fig. 10-4. Individual panels on the frieze on the front of the Ohio Supreme Court bench, from west to east. *A,* women's suffrage; *B,* county courthouses; *C,* the Treaty of Greenville; *D,* the passage of the Constitution of the United States in 1787; *E,* Ohio courthouses, represented by the early Marietta Courthouse; *F,* a gavel, as a symbol of courts; *G,* law books reflecting reliance on English common law; *H,* surveying equipment, referring to the many early legal disputes focused on property rights; *I,* a Supreme Court justice riding circuit to hear early cases; *J,* the Ohio Constitution; *K,* wagons with false bottoms and a lantern, as were used in the Underground Railroad; *L,* the Ohio Statehouse.

Above: Fig. 10–5. At the center of the Supreme Court bench is a stylized version of the seal of the Ohio Supreme Court.

Right: Fig. 10–6. The frieze of the Supreme Court bench is carved with the "egg and dart" pattern and at the edge with trillium flowers. At the bottom of the west side of the bench, Craig Vandall Stevens's signature emblem is a mouse, in place of one of the trillium flowers.

slaves fled from the South across the Ohio River into Ohio, most of them dispersing elsewhere.

The center panel on the bench is a stylized Supreme Court seal, also carved by Stevens (FIG. 10–5). It includes the traditional symbol for law and justice, the scale or balance. This carving differs from the official seal of the Ohio Supreme Court, which can be seen on the Front Street exterior (see FIG. 3–12, p. 32).

The frieze on the front and sides of the bench features a horizontal sculptured band with "egg and dart," a pattern of rimmed ovoids separated by blocks containing holes (FIG. 10–6). Above and below this design are trillium flowers, the state flower of Ohio. Since wood-carvers leave their signatures in their work, and the British furniture-maker Robert Thompson started using a mouse as his trademark in the 1920s, Craig Stevens carved the emblem of a small mouse in place of a trillium on the west side of the bench, with his initials ("CVS") under the ovoid and behind the tail of the mouse.

Chief Justice Moyer was committed to making the workings of the Ohio Supreme Court and the judicial system understandable to all people. The architects set aside space on the ground floor for a Visitor Education Center and, working with Jay Wuebbold, who was then the manager of civic education and outreach programs, created engaging displays and informative activities (see FIG. 4–1Z, p. 36). The Visitor Education Center tells of the Court's activities and explains some of the Court's decisions. Other displays describe important decisions in ways that are understandable for visitors (FIG. 10–7).

Fig. 10–7. Visitor Education Center on the ground floor, with interactive displays of important decisions and explanations of the judicial system.

Many visitors are schoolchildren, who learn about the judicial system by taking tours of the building. The entrance for school tours is on the ground floor, providing convenient access to a mock courtroom, which has a bench, jury box, and tables for the attorneys (FIG. 10–8). With guidance from staff, the students can experience the events of a trial.

As part of the renovation planning, the need for a law library was filled by using the space of the former State Library of Ohio, on the eleventh to fifteenth floors (FIG. 10–9). A new stairway was added from the twelfth to the thirteenth floor, featuring new bronze rails in an Art Deco style (FIG. 10–10).

With the new bookcases increasing the weight on the fourteenth floor, new structural supports were needed. Schooley Caldwell Associates came up with an Art Deco–style design to suspend the floor from the ceiling with bent metal "pretzels" attached to the steel beams of the fourteenth floor (FIG. 10–11).

The Rule of Law Gallery on the eleventh floor is an elongated gallery that leads from the elevators to the north into the Law Library reading room and has chairs for sitting and reading or appreciating the new paintings (FIG.

10–12). These works were created in 2004, 70 years after construction of the building, and represent an important addition to the building's internal art. Six large paintings depict the evolution of law in Western civilization as interpreted by an artist in the early 2000s. Ron Anderson, an artist from Columbus, Ohio, and instructor at Columbus College of Art and Design,

Right: **Fig. 10-8.** Visitor Education Center on the ground floor, showing the mock judicial chamber.

Below: **Fig. 10-9.** Elevator lobby of the thirteenth floor, looking south and showing in the background the fourteenth and fifteenth floors with shelves.

Fig. 10-10. New stairwell connecting the fourteenth floor to the thirteenth floor.

created these paintings. Anderson attended Kent State University and has received many commissions, recognitions, and awards. Anderson's paintings are found in numerous galleries, museums, theaters, and businesses in Ohio.

The paintings in the Rule of Law Gallery tell the history of law in the same fashion as the first-floor murals tell the history of Ohio. Here, through the lens of 2004, Anderson focuses on the struggles of people to gain access to the rule of law, rather than on the battles fought by political leaders for land, as depicted in the 1933 murals. The paintings in the Rule of Law Gallery begin in the southwest corner and continue to the north and around the room.

The first painting depicts, on the left half, the Code of Hammurabi, which dates from around 1750 BCE in Mesopotamia (FIG. 10-13A), laws written on large stones. On the right half is shown the lengthy rule of Ramses the Great, a prosperous ruler of Egypt. In the next painting, on the left side, is portrayed Draco, a legislator of ancient Greece, who replaced a system of oral law with a written court code around 600 BCE (FIG. 10-13B), and the right side portrays the Twelve Tables of Roman Law, which were

Right: **Fig. 10-11.** New floor supports in the Art Deco style hold the fourteenth floor to the ceiling.

Below: **Fig. 10-12.** Rule of Law Gallery, on the eleventh floor in the law library looking south to the elevator lobby.

inscribed on bronze in about 450 BCE. As shown, the Magna Carta was signed by King John of England in 1215 CE, an early proclamation of rights given by a ruler to their people (FIG. 10–13*C*). The US Constitution is shown being signed on September 17, 1787, setting out the framework for the US government (FIG. 10–13*D*). It was the first of its kind and remains a model for other nations today. The French Revolution is included, because it was the end of a monarchy and the beginning of a series of governments based on democracy (FIG. 10–13*E*). The last painting depicts an impartial Lady Justice leading the American people in the ongoing struggle for civil rights (FIG. 10–13*F*). As do many artists, Anderson included his own image in the painting at the lower right of this painting.

Another important part of the renovation was the addition of sculptures to the outdoor reflecting pools. Originally, the north and south reflecting pools served as a refreshing place to sit and relax, and they had no sculptures. During the renovation, Malcolm Cochran was commissioned to create art for the north reflecting pool (FIG. 10–14). He selected ten words that are

Fig. 10-13. Paintings in the Rule of Law Gallery. *A,* southwest corner, the Code of Hammurabi (*left*) and the rule of Ramses the Great (*right*); *B,* west side, Draco, the coder of law (*left*), and the twelve tablets of Roman law (*right*); *C,* northwest corner, the signing of the Magna Carta by King John of England; *D,* northeast corner, the signing of the American Constitution; *E,* east side, the French Revolution; *F,* southeast corner, the American civil rights struggle.

Fig. 10–14. North reflecting pool, looking north, showing the ten words of justice.

intrinsically related to the judicial system and used them in all capital letters: PEACE, TRUTH, JUSTICE, WISDOM, HONOR, HONESTY, REASON, EQUITY, COMPASSION, and INTEGRITY. The upper surfaces of the stone letters are just under the surface of the water, and sometimes with the water's movement they become blurry, as does the law. In addition, Cochran created a unique font for the letters used in the sculpture. Malcolm Cochran, a Columbus artist, was a faculty member at the Ohio State University and currently is on the faculty at the Columbus College of Art and Design. He has received commissions from throughout the country.

In the south reflecting pool, a very large gavel sculpture was added (FIG. 10–15). The artist, Andrew F. Scott, focuses on computer-based fabrication of sculpture. Scott earned his MFA from the Ohio State University and is currently a faculty member at the University of Texas at Dallas in the School of Arts, Humanities, and Technology. Scott wanted to create a large sculpture that would be seen by motorists driving past the building. Originally, he suggested plaques on either side of the sound block, reading "No Justice" and "No Peace." The plaques were considered too controversial and were not used.

There also is a new dedication plaque in the ground floor lobby (FIG. 10–16). Under an original bronze relief with two American Indian children, the top of the plaque contains the 2004 rededication of the building after renovation, and the bottom half honors Thomas J. Moyer (FIG. 4–5, p. 40)

The text on the plaque reads as follows:

Fig. 10–15. South reflecting pool, with gavel sculpture.

Overleaf: Fig. 10–16. Ground floor lobby, east wall, with bas-relief and dedication plaque.

The Supreme Court of Ohio
Ohio Judicial Center
2004
For the first time since it was established in 1803, the Supreme Court of Ohio occupies a building developed exclusively for the Judicial Branch of Ohio government. During its first century the Court was located in the Statehouse, then in 1901 moved into the Statehouse Annex (now called the Senate Building), sharing space with Legislative and Executive Branch agencies in both locations. Now, after leaving its home in the Rhodes State Office Tower and following a three-year renovation, the Court and affiliated offices reside in this newly dedicated home of the Judicial Branch. Built during 1930-33 as the Ohio Departments Building, this magnificent, historic building stands in recognition of the role of the judiciary as an independent, co-equal branch of government and reflects the commitment of the citizens of Ohio to the rule of law.
The Supreme Court of Ohio
Thomas J. Moyer, Chief Justice
Alice Robie Resnick, Justice
Francis E. Sweeney, Justice
Paul E. Pfeifer, Justice
Evelyn Lundberg Stratton, Justice
Maureen O'Connor, Justice
Terrence O'Donnell, Justice
State of Ohio
Bob Taft, Governor
Architect, 1929-1933
Harry Hake, Cincinnati
Restoration Architects & Engineers
Schooley Caldwell Associates, Columbus
Renovation Construction Manager
Messer Construction Company
A Project of the
Ohio Building Authority
Buildings housing the institutions of democracy should reflect the powerful belief of our citizens that government by the people is fundamental to the enjoyment of our lives. Our public buildings should inspire, engender respect, and enhance our trust. When one enters a court building, she should sense that something very special happens there: the peaceful, fair resolution of disputes. I can assure you, the new home for the Ohio judiciary certainly says that.
- Chief Justice Thomas J. Moyer, State of the Judiciary, September 11, 2003
IT IS HEREBY ORDERED by the SUPREME COURT OF OHIO, on this the 2nd day of December 2011:
The OHIO JUDICIAL CENTER shall hereafter be known as the
THOMAS J. MOYER OHIO JUDICIAL CENTER
in recognition of and dedication to the life and legacy of Chief Justice Thomas J. Moyer and his influence on the rule of law and administration of justice in the State of Ohio.
Maureen O'Connor, Chief Justice
Paul E. Pfeifer, Justice
Evelyn Lundberg Stratton, Justice
Terrence O'Donnell, Justice
Judith Ann Lanzinger, Justice
Robert R. Cupp, Justice
Yvette McGee Brown, Justice
OHIO

The Supreme Court of Ohio
Ohio Judicial Center
2004

For the first time since it was established in 1803, the Supreme Court of Ohio occupies a building developed exclusively for the Judicial Branch of Ohio government. During its first century the Court was located in the Statehouse, then in 1901 moved into the Statehouse Annex (now called the Senate Building), sharing space with Legislative and Executive Branch agencies in both locations. Now, after leaving its home in the Rhodes State Office tower and following a three-year renovation, the Court and affiliated offices reside in this newly dedicated home of the Judicial Branch. Built during 1930–33 as the Ohio Departments Building, this magnificent, historic building stands in recognition of the role of the judiciary as an independent, co-equal branch of government and reflects the commitment of the citizens of Ohio to the rule of law.

Supreme Court of Ohio
Thomas J. Moyer. Chief Justice

Alice Roble Resnick, Justice

Francis E. Sweeney, Justice

Paul E, Pfeifer, Justice

Evelyn Lundberg Stratton, Justice

Maureen O'Connor, Justice

Terrence O'Donnell, Justice

State of Ohio
Bob Taft, Governor

Architect, 1929–1933
Harry Hake, Cincinnati

Restoration Architects & Engineers
Schooley Caldwell Associates, Columbus

Renovation Construction Manager
Messer Construction Company

A Project of the
Ohio Building Authority

Buildings housing the Institutions of democracy should reflect the powerful belief of our citizens That government by the people is fundamental to the enjoyment of our lives. Our public buildings Should inspire, engender respect, and enhance our trust. When one enters a court building, she Should sense that something very special happens there: fair resolution of disputes. I can assure you, the new home for the Ohio Judiciary certainly says that.

—Chief Justice Thomas J. Moyer, State of the Judiciary. September 11, 2003

IT IS HEREBY ORDERED by the SUPREME COURT OF OHIO on this the 2nd day of December 2011:

The OHIO JUDICIAL CENTER shall hereafter be known as the
THOMAS J. MOYER OHIO JUDICIAL CENTER
In recognition of and dedication to the life and legacy of Chief Justice Thomas J. Moyer and his influence on the rule of law and administration of justice in the State of Ohio.

Paul E. Pfeifer, Justice
Judith Ann Lanzinger, Justice

Maureen O'Connor, Chief Justice
Evelyn Lundberg Stratton, Justice
Robert R. Cupp, Justice

Terrence O'Donnell, Justice
Yvette McGee Brown, Justice

Following the death of Chief Justice Thomas J. Moyer and to honor his lifelong record of judicial work, on December 2, 2011, the building was renamed the Thomas J. Moyer Ohio Judicial Center. As a nationally renowned jurist, Chief Justice Thomas J. Moyer was responsible for many efforts to strengthen Ohio law and for the relocation of the Ohio Judiciary to this building. The portrait of Chief Justice Moyer (see FIG. 6–13, p. 63) was placed where people entering the building could see it (FIG. 10–17). The portrait was made by Leslie Adams of Toledo, Ohio, a well-established portrait artist who studied at the New York Academy of Art. She has painted many Ohio leaders in government, universities, and corporations. The inscription below the portrait reads:

Thomas J. Moyer
Chief Justice Supreme Court of Ohio
January 1, 1987–April 2, 2010

Fig. 10–17. Portrait and dedication of the building to Chief Justice Thomas J. Moyer, located in the grand concourse.

In recognition of his commitment to the rule of law and his vision for an independent home for the judicial branch of Ohio government, this building is dedicated as the
Thomas J. Moyer Ohio judicial Center
December 2, 2011

The Honorable Maureen O'Connor was elected in 2010 as the first woman chief justice of the Ohio Supreme Court, and she retired in 2022. She also served both as a lieutenant governor and as an associate justice of the Ohio Supreme Court. The placement of Chief Justice Maureen O'Connor's portrait in the Grand Concourse is to honor her, for several reasons: as the first woman to serve as a chief justice of the Ohio Supreme Court, for her work in reforming Ohio law, and as the longest-serving elected official among all women in Ohio history (FIG. 10–18). Paul Wyse is the portrait artist. Wyse, from Cleveland, Ohio, is well known for his numerous portraits of prominent artists and corporate, government, and academic leaders.

Fig. 10–18. Portrait honoring retired Chief Justice Maureen O'Connor, located in the grand concourse.

The plaque under the portrait of the Honorable Maureen O'Connor reads:

Maureen O'Connor

First Woman Chief Justice
Supreme Court of Ohio
2011–2022

Associate Justice
2003–2010

To end this book about the Ohio Judicial Center, it is appropriate to restate the first sentence of the introduction: "Architecture captures the sum of the materials, craft, art, and vision that often outlive all of the artisans who participate in a structure's creation." The work and vision of both the original 1933 artists and those involved in the renovation are very much alive today and inspires our hope for Ohio's future.

ACKNOWLEDGMENTS

In the course of preparing this book, many people influenced its development and helped bring it into being. The biggest thanks go to Yvonne Burry for her editorial work and, importantly, for her encouragement on this project. A special thanks to Doreen Uhas-Sauer for sharing her love of history and editing the manuscript. Susan Wadsworth-Booth, director at Kent State University Press, understood this project and helped bring it to life. My thanks to Clara Totten and the staff of Kent State University Press, for making the publication a pleasure. Mason Farr made important comments on Ohio history after reviewing drafts of the early manuscript. Becky West of the Columbus Landmarks Foundation supplied strong encouragement when it was needed. For sharing her love of the building and helping with the photography, thanks to Sara Stiffler, Manager of Civic Education, Supreme Court of Ohio. Early development of the concept for the book involved conversations with Bob Loversidge, Anne and Tom Weeks, Lou Haskell, David Binkovitz, and Conrade Hinds. For their important interviews, I would like to thank Viggo B. A. Rambusch, Malcolm Cochran, Craig Vandall Stevens, Leslie Adams, Andrew F. Scott, and Robert Loversidge.

Research into the Ohio Judicial Center and Ohio history was aided by Elizabeth Woods at Ohio History Connection, Columbus, Ohio; Cynthia Prescott, PhD, Department of History and American Indian Studies, University of North Dakota, Grand Forks, North Dakota; Barbara Arnold of the Franklin Park Conservatory, Columbus, Ohio; Walter Eayrs of the Blackburn Building Conservation, Middleborough, Massachusetts; Barb Powers in the Ohio History Connection, Columbus, Ohio; and Stuart Hobbs, PhD, the Ohio State University, Columbus, Ohio.

Finally, I am indebted, for valuable conversations, to the following: Nancy Recchie and Jeff Darbee, for insights on publishing and building preservation; Ed Lentz, for his thoughts on history research; and Jeff

Clark, Esq, and Larry Sommers, for thoughtful remarks on drafts of the manuscript.

Most importantly, financial donations for help with publication are gratefully acknowledged from the following: Columbus Landmarks Foundation; Lee Shackelford, MD, philanthropist; Columbus Chapter of the American Institute of Architects, a professional organization; Schooley Caldwell, Bob Loversidge, FAIA, historic preservation; Robert V. Byrd, civic leader; and Charles C. Warner, Esq., leading senior attorney at the Porter Wright law firm.

SELECTED BIBLIOGRAPHY

The following list of works that were consulted as sources for this book is by no means a complete list of available information.

Published Sources

1788–1881 History of Washington County, Ohio with Illustrations and Biographical Sketches. Cleveland, OH: H. Z. Williams & Bro. Publishers, 1881.

Antal, Sandy. *A Wampum Denied: Procter's War of 1812.* 4th ed. Montreal: McGill–Queen's University Press, 2011.

Barry, John M. *The Great Influenza: The Story of the Deadliest Pandemic in History.* New York: Viking Press, 2005.

Bayer, Patricia. *Art Deco Architecture Design, Decoration and Detail from the Twenties and Thirties.* New York: Harry N. Abrams, 1992.

Brandt, Nat. *The Town That Started the Civil War.* Syracuse, NY: Syracuse University Press, 1991.

Breeze, Carla. *American Art Deco Architecture and Regionalism.* New York:
W. W. Norton & Company, 2003.

Dean, John W. *Warren G. Harding: The American Presidents Series; The 29th President, 1921–1923.* New York: Henry Holt and Company, 2004.

Falk, Peter H. *Rudolf Scheffler.* Madison, CT: Sound View Press, 1989.

Gampfer, Scott L. "Harry Hake Architects: Preserving the Records of an Eighty-Year Architectural Legacy at Cincinnati Museum Center." *Ohio Valley History* 15, no. 3 (2015): 78–83.

Greene, Karen, and Lynne Lavelle. *Art Deco Mailboxes: An Illustrated Design History.* New York: W. W. Norton & Company, 2014.

Harm, Gregory Paul. *Lee Lawrie's Prairie Deco: History in Stone at the Nebraska State Capitol.* 4th ed. Lincoln, NE: Bison Werks, 2011.

Hobbs, Stuart D. "Painting the Past: History, Memory, and Community in Modern Ohio." *Ohio History* 127, no. 2 (2020): 47–91.

Hurt, Douglas. *The Ohio Frontier Crucible of the Old Northwest, 1720–1830.* Bloomington: Indiana University Press, 1998.

Kern, Kevin F., and Gregory S. Wilson. *Ohio: A History of the Buckeye State.* Chichester, UK: John Wiley & Sons, 2014.

Knepper, George W. *Ohio and Its People.* Kent, OH: Kent State University Press, 1989.

Langsam, Walter E. *Biographical Dictionary of Cincinnati Architects, 1788–1940.* Cincinnati, OH: Architectural Foundation of Cincinnati, 2008.

Luebke, Frederick C., ed. *A Harmony of the Arts: The Nebraska State Capitol.* Lincoln: University of Nebraska Press, 1990.

McCullough, David. *The Pioneers—The Heroic Story of the Settlers Who Brought the American Ideal West.* New York: Simon & Schuster, 2019.

McLaughlin, Cynthia G. *The State Library at 200: A Celebration of Library Services to Ohio.* Brookfield, MO: Donning, 2017.

National Trust for Historic Preservation. *Walking Tour and Pocket History: Netherlands Plaza.* 2014.

Poore, Patricia. "Beaux-Arts Style, Architecture and Opulence of the American Renaissance, 1885–1930." *Old House Journal,* updated June 16, 2021, https://www.oldhouseonline.com/house-tours/beaux-arts-style.

Powers, Barbara. "Ohio's Pride: The Art and Architecture of the Ohio State Office Building." *Timeline* 23, no. 1 (2006): 2–19.

Rolfes, Steven J., and Douglas R. Weise. *Cincinnati Art Deco: Images of America.* Charleston, SC: Arcadia, 2014.

Stockwell, Mary. *The Other Trail of Tears: The Removal of the Ohio Indians.* Yardley, PA: Westholme, 2016.

Striner, Richard. *Art Deco.* New York: Abbeville Press, 1994.

Supreme Court of Ohio. *The Thomas J. Moyer Ohio Judicial Center.* Columbus, OH: Office of Public Information, 2013.

Wilson, James. *The Earth Shall Weep: A History of Native America.* New York: Grove Press, 1998.

Unpublished Sources

"Description of New Ohio State Office Building Columbus Ohio." Ohio Historic Archives Library, PA Box 85 13.

Hobbs, Stuart D., and Barbara Powers. "The Architecture and Art of the Ohio Courts Building." Unpublished manuscript, 2003. Typescript.

Schooley Caldwell Associates. *Ohio Judicial Center Dedication Ceremony.* Published in conjunction with the dedication of the renovated Ohio Judicial Center, May 15, 2004.

Schooley Caldwell Associates. *The Supreme Court of Ohio: Renovation of the Ohio Departments of Building Master Plan.* n.d. Printed document.

INDEX

Page numbers in **bold** denote images and associated captions.